DEATH AND ELIZABETHAN TRAGEDY

DEATH AND ELIZABETHAN TRAGEDY

A STUDY OF CONVENTION AND OPINION
IN THE ELIZABETHAN DRAMA

BY

THEODORE SPENCER

NEW YORK

PAGEANT BOOKS, INC.

1960

TO MY WIFE

PREFACE

THERE is no one fact in human experience that carries with it so many connotations or creates so many emotional vibrations as the fact of death. As soon as man becomes self-conscious he sees it as the dark, inevitable curtain against which all his actions are performed, and into the blackness of which he must in the end irrevocably be absorbed. Everyone knows that he must experience it, and emotion aroused by its contemplation is an emotion everyone can understand. The problems death implies are the central problems of life, and hence they are the central subject matter of art, of all that tries to comprehend and express those problems. Our conceptions of comedy and tragedy, our ideals of bravery, of beauty, of wisdom, our views of others and of ourselves, all depend on the fact of death, and were death suddenly abolished, not one of them would remain the same.

It is therefore obvious that a discussion like this, which attempts to define the attitudes toward death in a short period of time and to show how they affected dramatic poetry, cannot attempt to be complete even for the small field it is supposed to describe. It can only pick out what seems most important, and give hints which may possibly be illuminating. The subject has such wide implications that the student is tempted into making many digressions which must rigorously be suppressed. It would, for example, have been interesting to point out, as a background to this study, that to primitive man natural death seems an impossibility, and any conclusion to life the work of violence or a magician's spell; one would have liked to describe the notion of immortality such a belief involves, and to discuss its affinities with Homer's Hades and the Hebrew Sheol; it would have been illuminating to discuss how, to many cultivated people in classic times, the day of death was a conclusion to everything valuable, how they thought of it as "perfidus, infelix, horridusque," and how, if they imagined anything beyond, they could imagine only regret.

Indeed, this last opinion is worth emphasizing, for it is the natural opinion of mankind in those periods when an other-worldly religion has not covered it over with pictures of eternal torment or bliss. And it was the opinion which many people in the English Renaissance most wanted to give voice to. The men of the sixteenth century had a new confidence that the things of this world were valuable and noble. To them this classical point of view, which they found in the philosophy and literature Italy had displayed to them, expressed, in a way their still largely medieval paths of thought could not express, the sentiments that their apparent rediscovery of the world aroused. At that time it was felt, through some inexplicable resurgence of vitality, that man's brief mortal existence contained all that was necessary to satisfy his desires. Sensuous things were to be enjoyed for their own sakes, and a robust and harmonious expression of delight in worldly affairs was to be admired and pursued.

But such a feeling could not easily find a direct and serious expression. The tradition of the medieval past which taught the exact opposite, that man in the flesh was nothing and human life the valley of the shadow of death, was still too strong. A conflict between these two opposing attitudes to life was inevitable, and the result was not only drama in a technical, but also in a deeper, a psychological and sociological, sense. And this conflict, which is felt by every age with varying degrees of intensity, was expressed more vividly for a few years during the English Renaissance (from about 1588 to about 1620) than for a long time before or since. The vision of all its implications contributed to the greatness of Shakespeare and the greatness of the literature which surrounded him. It was a literature which was aware of the central emotional problems of human life, and this means that it was a literature which, at one period in its development at least, made much of death.

An interesting feature of the conflict which produced this concentration is the fact that it took

place, so to speak, in the open. It was not an intellectual problem, to be argued about in the universities; it was an emotional problem that mattered
to everybody, and it was exhibited in the most
popular form of literature. We are thus in an un-
usually strong position when we take the drama as
the basis for any conclusions about the Elizabethan mind. For the Elizabethan plays were not
the product of brains which had only themselves
to please. The audience may not have immediately
caught the full meaning of *Faustus* and *Hamlet*, but
the courtier and shopkeeper who first saw such
plays must to some degree have shared the seriousness of their authors or they would not have been
performed or even written, and their popularity
shows that they reflected and probably influenced
the feelings of those who went so repeatedly to see
them.

These feelings, as I have said, were largely the
result of a long tradition. Hence I shall preface
my remarks on the Elizabethan attitude to death
by a discussion of medieval teaching on the subject;
I shall then try to show how this was affected by
the new interests of the sixteenth century; and
coming to the drama itself — abandoning, for a
time, the chronological approach — I shall discuss
its treatment of death in three ways: (1) as it affects
words, (2) as it affects ideas, (3) as it affects dramatic technique. The work will end with a return

to the chronological method, and I shall try to show the significance, for a history of the English Renaissance mind, of the opinions about death which were expressed by the major Elizabethan dramatists.

I have not tried to cover the material exhaustively; to have done so would have been to produce an enormous volume in which the critical suggestions and the accounts of general tendencies — my chief interest — would have been suffocated. But I hope that the many quotations and examples which I have not used, and which will undoubtedly occur to students of the period, will only serve to illustrate the points I have already made.

The subject of this book was first suggested to me by a sentence in Mr. T. S. Eliot's essay, "The Possibility of a Poetic Drama": "There is a book to be written on the commonplaces of any great dramatic period, the handling of Fate or Death, the recurrence of mood, tone, situation." My attention was caught by the possibilities implied in this remark; I began to collect the Elizabethan references to death, they were arranged with comments into a form suitable for a dissertation, and rearranged, finally, to form the present volume.

Professor G. L. Kittredge, Professor J. T. Murray, and Professor J. S. P. Tatlock were kind enough to read the manuscript in its earlier form, and to consider it worthy of passing certain official require-

ments. I am most grateful to Professor F. O. Matthiessen, Dr. W. E. Sedgwick, and Mr. Harry Levin
for their helpful criticism while the material was
being prepared for publication.

T. S.

ELIOT HOUSE
CAMBRIDGE, MASS.
January, 1936

CONTENTS

DEATH AND ELIZABETHAN TRAGEDY

Chapter I

THE MEDIEVAL BACKGROUND

O poggi, O valli, O fiume, O selve, O campi,
O testimon della mia grave vita,
Quante volte m'udiste chiamar, Morte!

Petrarch

I

MORE than any other period in history, the late Middle Ages were preoccupied with the thought of death. In Northern Europe for two hundred years — from the middle of the fourteenth century to the middle of the sixteenth — death was the favorite topic of preachers and moralistic writers, it was one of the most common subjects for popular art, and if a man of the period followed the prevailing doctrine, there was no object so frequently or so vividly before his mind's eye as the skeleton he would one day become.

Consequently if we are to understand the Elizabethan attitude to the subject in all its far-reaching and fascinating complications, we must have as clear as possible a picture of this late medieval background. In more ways than one, consciously and unconsciously, it influenced Elizabethan thought, and without it the Elizabethan mind, and its product Elizabethan literature, would have been a very different thing from what it was. The meditations of Hamlet, the bitterness of Flamineo — in fact a large proportion of the thoughts and actions of all Elizabethan heroes and villains in relation to death — have their roots in medieval teaching on the subject, a teaching that survived well into the time of Shakespeare. A dance of death decorated Shakespeare's parish church at Stratford-on-Avon, the prostitutes he met on the London streets were likely to have death's-head rings on their middle fingers, and if he ever listened to sermons, he could not avoid hearing the inherited teaching about death expounded again and again. We must therefore begin our study by examining the origins and history of that teaching, and we must try, however briefly, to describe and perhaps explain the unique and striking phenomena which were its expression.

To despise human life, to contemplate death and to think continually of the other world were not, of course, doctrines that had been invented by the Middle Ages. The philosophy of Plato, which taught that true reality lay outside the shadowy world of the senses, the metaphysical hierarchy of the neo-Platonists, which virtually identified evil with matter, the teaching of the Stoics, who were compelled to face the worldly ills they did their best to deny, the visions of Near-Eastern ascetics, who elaborated with increasing fervency of detail the tortures or delights of the next world — all these things had made men look forward to death, and had prepared the way for a scorn of man's natural abilities and an emphasis on the next world which should be the only satisfactory attitude for serious minds to maintain.

But Christianity added one remarkable doctrine which pagan disillusionment and transcendental philosophy had never mentioned. It taught that death was a punishment for man's sin. This was a notion entirely foreign to Greece and Rome; as Lessing remarked, "to deem death a punishment, could not of itself have occurred to the brain of a man who only used his reason, without revelation." To a Greek, life might be a punishment; the Orphics had said so when they remarked that the soul was sent down into the prison of the body because of some previously incurred fault; [1] but death was no penalty — far from it; it was a welcome release of the soul from its earthly bonds. "Hasten thy coming, death, lest I too forget myself," [2] exclaimed Marcus Aurelius; death to him was only a moment's unpleasantness, to be thought of as little as possible, and to be welcomed with a sigh, almost of relief.

1. See Plato, *Cratylus*, 400b (trans. Jowett): "For some say that the body is the grave of the soul which may be thought to be buried in our present life . . . probably the Orphic poets were the inventors of the name, and they were under the impression that the soul is suffering the punishment of sin, and that the body is an enclosure or prison in which the soul is incarcerated."

2. *Meditations*, IX, 3.

But when death was considered a punishment, it became at once the most critical moment of life. To think of death was to think of sin, and to think of sin was the only way to purify the soul. Death was no longer merely a step across a threshold or the closing of a door, it was the crucial event in human experience. By the fear of death, says St. Cyprian (200–258 A.D.), almost at the beginning of Christian teaching,

the lukewarm are inflamed, the slack are nerved up, the slothful are stimulated, the deserters are compelled to return, the heathens are constrained to believe, the ancient congregation of the faithful is called to rest, the new and abundant army is gathered to the battle with a graver vigor, to fight without fear of death when the battle shall come.[3]

At the same time it became necessary not only to emphasize the moment of death itself, but also to describe as vividly as possible the state in which the soul might find itself afterwards. Consequently we find visionary descriptions of hell and heaven very early in Christian history.[4] There is a horrifying

3. *De Mortalitate*, sec. 15, trans. R. E. Wallis, Edinburgh, 1868.
4. The most important of the early visions is the so-called *Apocalypse of Peter* (ed. J. A. Robinson and M. R. James, London, 1892), the date of which has been put at 150 A.D. We have a description of hell in the third century *Apocalypse of Paul*, a work of great popularity throughout the Middle Ages (see T. Silverstein, *Visio Sancti Pauli*, London, 1935), and in the fourth century *Sibylline Oracles*. These works are translated in M. R. James, *The Apocryphal New Testament*, Oxford, 1924, 505 ff. With the establishment of the doctrine of purgatory by Gregory the Great, a new development takes place, and the fiery details that were formerly the property of

veracity about these visions; even in the crudest of them we feel a certainty of detail which is lacking in the Homeric description of Hades, the somewhat conventionalized pictures of the other world that survive in the Orphic fragments, or the Hebrew descriptions of Sheol. Death, to the sinful, can only bring torment; it is no longer the end, but the beginning of true life. "Vale, vale, dulcissima, sem-

hell are given to the new locality. The pains of purgatory are described in Bede (*Eccl. Hist.*, v, 12); an Italian boy named Alberic experienced them in the twelfth century (F. Cancellieri, *Osservazione . . . sopra l'originalità . . . di Dante*, Rome, 1814, pp. 162 ff.); Barontus of the "monasterium S. Petri Longoretense" in France, also tells about them (*Mon. Germ. Hist.*, Script. Rerum Merovingicarum, Hanover, 1910, v, 368–394); and Matthew Paris relates three similar accounts (*Chronica Maior*, Owayn, 1153 A.D., the monk of Eynsham, 1196 A.D., and Thurcill, 1206 A.D.). There are many others, but the most significant and popular of these visions were the vision of Tundale (O. F. version ed. V.-H. Friedel and K. Meyer, Paris, 1907), and the adventures of Sir Owayn in St. Patrick's Purgatory (M. E. version in C. Horstmann, *Early South-English Legendary*, E. E. T. S. [1887], pp. 199 ff.). These are supposed to date, respectively, from 1149 and 1153. Their popularity was phenomenal; of Tundale's vision there exist fifty-four Latin manuscripts alone (see A. Wagner, *Visio Tnugdali*, Erlangen, 1882), not to mention translations into French, English, Italian, Irish, and Icelandic.

It is interesting to note that in only a small minority of these visions is hell described, and of course the pleasures of paradise with which many of them close are very feebly pictured as compared with the torments of purgatory. Though hell was by no means forgotten, purgatory was a place of greater immediacy to the average man, and his life could be better improved by thinking about its terrors. Dante's description of purgatory and his salutation of the souls in durance there as "O ben finiti, O gia spiriti eletti" (*Purg.*, III, 73) give an entirely different impression from the descriptions we have in the earlier visions.

per in perpetuo vale," might be carved on a Roman tombstone; the Christian, either in hope or in despair, would say a very different thing. The lesson taught by Abbot Evagrius to the monks under his charge, that they should think continually of death and the pains of hell — "never forget these things, whether in thy cell or without —" [5] this lesson became the universally accepted teaching throughout the Christian centuries. One must continually despise the present life, meditate on death as a punishment for sin, think of the moment of death as one of extreme importance, and contemplate the tortures of the other world.

2

But it was a long time before this teaching, all centering in the fact that death is a punishment for sin, became vivified by emotion. No one questioned it, it was earnestly recommended by all religious writers, but with the exception of the descriptions of hell, it was rarely brought home by vivid examples or by impassioned feeling. For example, much is said about death in the well-known *Vers de la Mort* of Hélinant, which were written between 1194 and 1197, yet even his most effective stanzas (xx-xxxiii), describing death's universality, are a collection of

5. *Vitaspatrum*, I, col. 862, quoted by G. G. Coulton, *Five Centuries of Religion*, Cambridge, England, 1923, I, 99.

abstractions, admirably expressed as they are; they affect us intellectually, they lack the "human touch" which the later Middle Ages were so successfully to develop. This is also true of an exactly contemporary work, the *De Contemptu Mundi* [6] of Pope Innocent III, in which the author sets out, purely by force of logic, to humble man's pride with a description of the vileness of the human condition and the horrors of death. We do not feel, as we read his words, that Innocent was moved very strongly by what he had to say: the miseries of mankind only touched his brain, not his heart, and he described them unemotionally, with a kind of jaunty wit, which to a modern reader almost defeats its object.[7]

If we move on, however, a hundred and fifty years later and examine another work which says very much the same thing, we notice a remarkable difference. *The Pricke of Conscience* [8] (*circa* 1340), attributed until recently to Richard Rolle, devotes much space to describing the importance and the horrors of death, and it describes them with as much emotion as the author has at his command. The intellectual, the almost jocose logical thoroughness of

6. Ed. J. H. Achterfeldt, Bonn, 1855.

7. It is sometimes difficult to believe that Innocent took all his arguments seriously. Here is one of them. Consider, he says, the trees and the herbs of the field; they produce balsam and scent, oil and wine. But what does man produce? "Sputum, urinam et stercus." As is the fruit, so is the tree (i, 9). The conclusion, Innocent would have us believe, is inescapable.

8. Ed. R. Morris, Berlin, 1863.

Innocent has gone; everything is in deadly emotional earnest.

> Ded is the mast dred thing that es
> in all this world,

the author begins,[9] and not bodily death alone, but the death of the spirit when it is separated from God, and the endless death which is the death of hell. When a man dies, he has two pains:

> Ane es for the payne that a man has,
> When the dede hym assayls, and slas.
> The tother es, for when his lif sal here ende,
> He what never whider he sal wende.

The moment of death, when the soul parts from the body, is indeed the most dread thing in the world. Imagine the human body a soil in which a tree is planted, a root stretching down into every vein and nerve and sinew, a growing part of each; when death comes, it is as if this tree were torn out by the roots from the body where it grows. Yet even this is the least of the pains to be endured at death, and the fear of this is only the first of the fears which accompany it. It is to be feared, in the second place, for the sight of the devils that will appear about the dying body;

> For when the lyf sal pas fra a man
> Devels sal gadir obout hym than,
> To ravissche the saul with tham away
> Tyl pyne of helle, if thai may.

9. Vv. 1666 ff.

They will make horrid noises and faces like mad lions, they will try to bring the dying man into despair by threatenings and fear of the hopelessness of his sins.[10] They will surely come, for they came to St. Martin when he died, and to St. Bernard. It is impossible to imagine how horrible they are; no living man could bear the sight of them, hence they only come at death;

> Bot when the ded assaylles a man,
> In the foulest figure thai apere than;
> Tharfor aght ilk man dredand be
> Agayne the tyme when he sal tham se.[11]

The third pain of death comes with the recollection of one's past life; the devils recite one's evil

10. See the M. E. *Gesta Romanorum*, ed. S. J. H. Herrtage, E. E. T. S. (1879), no. 88, for the story of a repentant swearer who despaired, thinking his sins too great to be forgiven, and so went to hell.

11. This is not the only poem which refers to these devils. We are told in *The Ayenbite of Inwit* that when death comes, "A thouzend dyevlen ssolle come myd hire, and brenge mid ham greate bokes and bernynde hokes and chaynen avere" (ed. R. Morris, E. E. T. S. [1866], p. 264). When the pope Celestin was about to die, a thousand devils came to take him ("Celestin," ed. C. Horstmann, *Anglia*, 1 [1877–78], 55 ff.). In the "Debate of the Body and the Soul," the sinful spirit hears the hounds of hell yelling for him,

> "And fendes mo than men mowe se,
> That comen to fette me to helle;"

horrible black creatures, ragged, hump-backed, with sharp claws and long nails (E. Mätzner, *Altenglische Sprachproben*, Berlin, 1867, 1, 100, vv. 355 ff.). The *Gesta Romanorum* tells a story of how four devils appeared to a dying man (*ed. cit.*, no. 83); Caesarius of Heisterbach relates several unquestionable anecdotes of a similar nature. The following is perhaps worth quoting (a demon deeds, and angels appear (the first palliating circumstance) to recite one's good deeds. You will see, says the poet, quoting St. Anselm, all your hideous unshriven sins appearing before you. How many these may be, who knows? St. Bernard found his whole life sinful; what will it be for a really wicked man? And then comes the last dread of all. What will happen when the soul is uprooted, and the sins have been taken into account? Will the grinning

---

is talking to a knight, describing a deathbed scene he had just attended): "We were more in number than the sands of the sea. Yet we got but little profit; for those lousy monks grovelled all round him, grunting out their psalms like pigs, and suffered us not to come near. . . ." Then said the knight, "Fool! how didst thou dare to come to the deathbed of so just a man?" "Dare?" said he, "Why I was present when the son of God breathed his last, sitting on the arm of the cross!" (ed. J. Strange, Cologne, 1851, ii, 319). In a fourteenth-century poem called *The Gast of Guy*, the return ghost, when asked what thing is most terrifying at the time of death, replies,

> "the syght sall mast him dere
> Of foule fendes, that him wald fere,
> For than thai sall obout him be
> Defygurd all in foule degre,
> And grysely sall thai gryn and gnayst
> Out of his witt him for to wrayst."

(Ed. G. Schleich, Berlin, 1898. [*Palaestra* I], vv. 601 ff.).

Even the Virgin Mary when she dies has to endure this experience. In the play of the death of Mary in the York cycle, though she prays to be spared the sight of the devil, Mary is answered by the voice of her son:

> "Bot modir, the fende muste be nedis at thyne endying,
>   In figoure full foule for to fere the"

(*York Plays*, ed. Lucy Tolmin Smith, Oxford, 1885, "The Death of Mary," vv. 154 ff.).

black devils snatch it (as they did in the "Debate of the Body and the Soul"), and carry it jubilantly away, cutting it with red-hot ploughshares and pricking it with burning flesh-hooks? Who can say? Therefore it is above all essential to think of your ending day, and be ready for it with a good life. As St. Augustine says, every man

> Shuld haf drede of hys last day;

follow Solomon's advice, and "Thynk on thi endy-ing day —" "Thynk thou sal dyghe, thou wate never whan,"

> Tharfor at morne, when thou sese lyght,
> Thynk als thou sal dygh ar nyght:

let the thought of death never be absent from your mind, so that you may be prepared for it when it comes.[12]

12. The only one of the four pains of death described by this writer which apparently bears a resemblance to reality is that which speaks of the remembrance of past acts. Mr. R. S. Ellis in an article, "The Attitude toward Death and the Types of Belief in Immortality; a study in the Psychology of Religion," in *Journal of Religious Psychology*, VII (1915), 466–510, has given the results taken from numerous accounts by people who lost consciousness from accident or severe illness. Their sensations of lapsing into blankness must be close to those which accompany actual death. These sensations, Mr. Ellis reports, are, like our author's, four — but of an entirely different nature to those the medieval poet describes. First there is a feeling which can only be described as one of beatitude; second, an anesthesia of touch combined with unusual acuity of hearing and sight; third, an unusual rapidity of thought and imagination; fourth, a recollection of past life. There is no sadness, according to Mr. Ellis's accounts, and an entire absence of fear and pain.

3

Such teaching was beginning to be very common all over Europe in the fourteenth century, and it would be an easy matter to collect quotation after quotation to exemplify it. But as we read over this long and elaborate description, in which the poet has used all the art at his command to make death as emotionally terrible as he can, and as we compare it with the cold-blooded rationality of Innocent's remarks on exactly the same subject, several perplexing questions come to mind. What has caused the change? Why should a doctrine that had been accepted for over a thousand years take on at this period a new form, and be felt with an intensity and freshness that it had never known before? Was there anything in the background or the atmosphere of the fourteenth century which would make this emotional emphasis on death plausible and sympathetic?

These are not easy questions to answer, and to answer them fully would take us far outside the limits imposed by our subject. For the fourteenth century emphasis on death is only one symptom of a change that took place in every form of human thought and feeling as the Middle Ages advanced: it is a change that affected Christianity as a whole, not merely this one doctrine. With the development of the Middle Ages, from the end of the twelfth century on, the objects of Christian devotion — the Virgin and Child, the Crucifixion, the figures of the saints — became more and more realistically portrayed, and with the increasing realism came an increased emphasis on emotion. Everyone knows, for example, that the Virgin and Child as presented in twelfth-century sculpture is a very different thing from the Virgin and Child as presented in the sculpture of the fourteenth century. In the first we see a wooden figure, a miniature adult, standing stiffly on his mother's knees, holding his hand out in a formal gesture of benediction. He is not a child — he is the embodiment of a doctrine. But by the fourteenth century, with the growth of realism, the doctrine has disappeared: in the many charming statues and pictures which have survived from that period, we see a real child turning naturally to look up at his mother's face, a child who may be playing with a bird, or who has fallen asleep over a book. We no longer think of a God mysteriously become man; we are brought down to earth, and we feel for the child almost as if it were our own.

This appeal to emotion by an attempt at realistic portrayal of the objects of emotion marks more than anything else the first steps of the Renaissance. Indeed if we consider the development of the European mind from this point of view, all its various changes from the time of St. Bernard of Clairvaux (1095–1155) to the time of Shakespeare may be seen as parts of one unbroken movement, and the creation of Hamlet may be regarded as a remote consequence of St. Bernard's contemplation of the sufferings of Christ. In desiring to get nearer to God, man made God more and more like himself, and there finally came a time when realism, at first connected inextricably with religion, was used for its own sake. What we call the Renaissance began at that moment.

St. Bernard's influence on medieval emotion, and hence on the emotion which followed the Middle Ages, was enormous. He taught men how to feel in a new way, which, when the objects of contemplation are standardized, is more important than teaching them how to think in a new way, and the cult of the Virgin, which was one of the forms that new feeling took, gained its chief impetus from him. Equally significant for later generations, and more important for our present purpose, was the emphasis he put on the human pains of Jesus.

I, brethren, from the beginning of my conversion, set myself, in place of all the merits in which I knew that I was wanting, to bind up this little bundle of myrrh [13] for my individual needs, collected from all the cares and bitter experiences of my Lord, and to keep it always close upon my breast; in the first place of the privations of His infant years; then of the labours

---

13. The text of the sermon is "A bundle of myrrh is my well-beloved unto me" (*Cant.*, I, 13). I quote from the translation by S. J. Eales, *Life and Works of St. Bernard*, London, 1896, IV, Sermon XLIII, sec. 3.

He underwent in preaching, His fatigues in journeying to and fro, His watchings in prayer, His fastings and temptations, His tears of compassion, the snares laid for Him in discourse; and, lastly, of His perils among false brethren, of insults, spitting, blows, abuse, scorn, piercing by nails, and other such things, which He suffered for the salvation of our race. . . . To meditate on these things I have called wisdom; in these I have placed the perfection of righteousness for me, the fulness of knowledge, the abundance of merits, the riches of salvation. There is among them for me sometimes a draught of salutary bitterness; sometimes, again, a sweet unction of consolation. . . . I have these [sufferings of Jesus] frequently in my mouth, as you know, and always in my heart, as God knows. . . . In a word, my philosophy is this, and it is the loftiest in the world: to know JESUS, and Him crucified.[14]

St. Francis emphasized still further the importance of such a philosophy,[15] and was rewarded by having the marks of Christ's sufferings inflicted on his own body. His disciples carried his teachings all over Europe, and at the end of the thirteenth century they were embodied in a very interesting work,

14. See, for the same thing, Bernard's "Sermo de Passione Domini," *Opera*, I, coll. 1942–44, quoted by R. S. Storrs, *Bernard of Clairvaux*, New York, 1892, p. 184. Here too the sorrows of Christ are insisted on.

15. Francis, "drunk with love and compassion of Christ, . . . picked up a branch from the earth and laying it on his left arm, he drew in his right hand another stick like a bow over it, as if on a viol or other instrument, and making fitting gestures, sang with it in French unto the Lord Jesus Christ. But all this playing ended in tears, and this joy dissolved in compassion for the Passion of Christ. In these times he would draw sighs continually; and with deep drawn groans, forgetful of those things which he held in his hands, he was raised to Heaven." (*Speculum Perfectionis*, cap. xcɪɪɪ; see also cap. xcɪɪ. There are many similar stories.)

a kind of holy novel, the *Meditationes Vitae Christi*,[16] which was extremely popular, and which illustrates clearly the growing tendency toward realism.

In it we are given the most intimate details about Christ's birth, his childhood and, above all, his crucifixion. The manner of his scourging, the wounds made by the crown of thorns, the fresh bleeding caused when his clothes, which had begun to stick to his wounds, were torn off that he might be crucified — all are presented with the most vivid detail. We are told exactly how the cross was set up on the "stinking (*foetidum*) hill of Calvary," how Christ's body was nailed to it by men standing on ladders, and how as the cross, with Christ on it, was set down into the hole prepared for it, all his sinews were jarred and broken.

Everywhere his most sacred blood flowed out in streams from his great wounds. He was so tortured that he could move no part of his body but his head. There three nails sustained the weight of his whole body, and he suffered the most bitter anguish and torment, more than can be thought or told.[17]

And the author repeatedly urges us, as we read these descriptions, to picture them so vividly in our minds

16. The Latin text may be found in the folio edition of Bonaventura's works printed at Lyons, 1668, vol. VI. It was translated, very freely, into English verse by Robert Mannyng of Brunne, *circa* 1315–30, and again, with more faithfulness to the original, though by no means literally, into prose by Nicholas Love, in 1410. The English versions have been several times reprinted.

17. Cap. LXXVIII.

that we shall weep as if we had been present at the scene itself.

Until the close of the thirteenth century emotion of this kind about the Passion of Christ had ordinarily been held in check. St. Anselm, for example, did not weep at the thought of the crucifixion, because just as he was about to be moved, he decided that he ought rather to rejoice on account of the benefits the crucifixion had brought with it.[18] And during the time of St. Thomas Aquinas intellectual interests were too keen to be overruled by emotion: the *Divine Comedy* was possible because feeling and thought were for a brief time at the same level of intensity.

But the precarious marriage between the rationalism of Aristotle and the Passion of Christ which made the greatness of the thirteenth century was bound to end in divorce; as the power of the intellect went astray and spent itself in futilities, the emotional emphasis was made top-heavy, it grew frantic, and ended in morbidity. M. Mâle has clearly shown how religious art, striving to be increasingly effective, pictured Christ with more and more evidences of suffering upon his person. The crown of thorns appeared for the first time at the beginning of the fourteenth century; by 1370 it was depicted as very weighty and painful, pressing down upon

18. Migne, *Pat. Lat.*, CLVIII, col. 675, quoted by E. Mâle, *L'Art Religieux de la Fin du Moyen Age en France*, Paris, 1925, p. 89.

Christ's head and wounding it. Soon realistic half-length pictures of Christ showing his wounds were to be found everywhere; [19] there were many religious poems in all languages for which such pictures might be literal illustrations:

> Loke to thi loverd, man, thar hanget he a rode,
> and wep hyf tho mist terres al of blode.
> Vor loke hu his heued biis mid thornes bi-wnde,
> and to his neb so bispet and to the spere-wnde.
> Faluet his feyre luer, and delewet his sicte,
> drowepet his hendi bodi that on rode biis itiht.
> Blickied his brest nacked and bledet hiis side,
> stiviet hiis arms that istreid beth so wide.
> Loke to the nailes on honde and on fete,
> hu the stremes hurned of that blod suete.
> Bigin at his molde and loke to his to,
> ne saltu no wit vinde bute anguisse and wo.[20]

And a fourteenth-century mystic, Juliana of Norwich, desiring to be joined in ecstasy with God, based her experience on images of a similar kind:

After this Christ shewed a part of His Passion near His dying. I saw His sweet face as it were dry and bloodless with pale dying. And later, more pale, dead, languoring; and then turned more dead unto blue; and then more brown-blue, as the flesh turned more deeply dead. . . . Thus I saw the sweet flesh dry in seeming by part after part, with marvellous pains. And as long as any spirit had life in Christ's flesh, so long suffered He pain.[21]

---

19. Mâle, *op. cit.*, pp. 100–101, 109 ff.

20. Early fourteenth century. From St. John's Coll. Camb. Ms. 15, printed in Carleton Brown, *Religious Lyrics of the Fourteenth Century*, Oxford, 1924, p. 2. See also pp. 50, 68, 94, etc.

21. *Revelations of Divine Love*, by Juliana of Norwich, ed. Grace

4

I have mentioned this emphasis on the Passion of Christ for two reasons. In the first place I believe that the development of realism and emotion it illustrates is the fundamental cause for the concentration on death which is one of the most notable facts about the later Middle Ages; and in the second place, it seems very likely that the continued contemplation of Christ's death made the individual contemplate, with increasing fervor, his own. In every movement there comes a time when the limit of feeling about essentials has been reached, and the means that were first used only towards an end higher than themselves either become empty formulas or vehicles for emotional dissipation. As we shall see, this occurred in the Elizabethan drama, and it also occurred in Christian Europe during the fourteenth century; people's minds became jaded, and the old teaching about death, because it made such a direct appeal to the emotions, grew more and more to be one of the most vital parts of Christianity.

Warrack, London, 1901, chap. xvi. The visions occurred in 1373. See also chap. x. Many similar descriptions could be quoted. There is a striking one in Sir Thomas More's *Dyalogue of Comforte* (1534), bk. III, chap. 27: "The consideracion of ye paynfull death of Christ, is sufficient to make us content to suffer paynfull death for his sake."

It would be tedious to enumerate or to quote at any length the various works which exemplify this teaching. The *Horologium Sapientiae* (1334) of the German mystic Suso, the *Ayenbite of Inwit* (1340), *The Craft of Deyng* (written at the end of the fourteenth century), Occleve's *Lerne to Dye* (early fifteenth century) — a translation of Suso — the *Opusculum Tripartitum* (before 1409) of Gerson, the enormously popular *Ars Moriendi*, which derived from Gerson and was known everywhere in Europe by the middle of the fifteenth century — all these works emphasize the overwhelming importance of death, and strongly urge their readers to keep the terrible thought of it always present in their minds.[22]

22. Book II, chap. 2, of Suso's *Horologium Sapientiae* is devoted to death. For Occleve's indebtedness to it see B. P. Kurtz, "The Relation of Occleve's *Lerne to Dye* to its Source," *P. M. L. A.*, XL (1925), 252 ff. There is a later English prose translation (early fifteenth century) of Suso, printed in F. M. Comper, *The Book of the Craft of Dying*, London, 1917, fourth selection. The *Ayenbite of Inwit*, which translates the French *Somme des Vices et des Vertues* (1279), is edited by R. Morris, E. E. T. S. (1866). *The Craft of Deyng* was edited for the E. E. T. S. by G. G. Perry (1866). For the *Ars Moriendi* see *The Ars Moriendi* (*Editio Princeps, circa* 1450); *A Reproduction of the Copy in the British Museum*, ed. W. H. Rylands, Holbein Society, London, 1881. The illustrations are also reproduced in F. P. Weber, *Aspects of Death*, London, 1918, pp. 96 ff. This work was translated into nearly all the European languages, and two abridgments of it were printed by Caxton. See E. Mâle, *op. cit.*, pp. 380 ff.; also Comper, *op. cit.*, preface. There were three main versions: the Latin *Ars Moriendi*, the later block books (some of the earliest examples of printing), and the French *L'Art de bien Vivre et bien Mourire*. For further discussion of the late medieval emphasis on death see J. Huizinga, *The Waning of the Middle Ages*, London, 1924.

Similar teaching is repeated everywhere in vernacular literature,

> Man wi niltu the bi cnowen,
> man wi niltu the bi see,
> of felthe thou art comen.
> wermes fode thu salt be.[23]

We hear the melancholy cry continually;

Memento homo quod cinis es et in cinerem reverteris,[24]

Memento, homo, quod cinis es! . . . Think, man, exceptioun thair is none, sed tu in cinerem reverteris.[25]

Death increasingly became the chief fact which the layman should associate with religion. And when it was so important, there was one thing particularly to be avoided, a sudden death; to die suddenly was to be deprived of all the rites of the Church. Without the religious *viaticum*, those black devils which hovered about every deathbed would have it all their own way, and the miserable soul would be hurried off to hell; hence fear of sudden death was a commonplace. Chaucer's Aurelius speaks of "sodein deth horrible"; [26] Lydgate, somewhat later, when writing about Antiochus, who was mad, despitious, cowardly, deceitful, and false, asks:

23. "Long Life," ed. J. Zupitza, *Anglia*, 1 (1877–78), 411–412, vv. 31 ff.
24. *Erthe upon Erthe*, ed. Hilda M. R. Murray, E. E. T. S. (1911), B version, 1, 21.
25. *Bannatyne MS.*, Hunterian Club, London, 1896, 11, 127.
26. *Canterbury Tales*, F 1010.

What was his eende? a sodeyn deth, parde,
For his outrages of pride & lecherie.[27]

This emphasis occurs, of course, in more specifically religious writers than Chaucer or Lydgate. We
find it in Bromyard's *Summa Praedicantium*, a once
popular, but now forgotten, collection of anecdotes
and moral sermons got together before 1390 (the ap-
proximate year of Bromyard's death) for the benefit
of Dominican preachers. "Men say," says Bromyard, "so long as our tongue can say three words [*in
manus tuas*] before our death, we shall escape all these
perils and snares of the devil!" But Bromyard has a
ready answer, in the form of anecdotes, to such remarks. "A certain man, who was wont to speak
thus, plunged on horseback, hot from hunting, into
a stream beyond his depth; he fell forthwith into the
water, and the three last words that he spake were,
'Devil take me!'" Another man could only speak
of his hunting dogs as he died; naturally he was
swept away to hell. Therefore, says Bromyard, with
these examples before us, "Let every man think in
his heart, how he will do when he is set in the midst
of his enemies; when he shall see the demons with
their hellish claws in readiness to seize upon his

27. *Fall of Princes*, bk. v, vv. 1612 ff. See a later poem, "The
Hye Way to the Spytell Hous," which says of those who are adulterous: "Eyther they shall be poore, or dye sodeynly" — a curious
mingling of worldly and religious values (Utterson, *Select Pieces of
Early Popular Poetry*, London, 1825, ii, 755 ff.).

soul." [28]   Bromyard, indeed, devotes 75 double-column quarto pages (in the edition of 1586, ii, foll. 48–86) to the discussion of death, treating the subject from every possible angle and ramming home his points with anecdotes. His work was the best known of the preachers' handbooks which were so common in the late Middle Ages, and there are many manuscripts of it; excerpts were made of it and widely circulated as brochures among the people; it was first printed in 1485, and then reprinted several times in the century that followed. Its emphasis on death and the horrors that attend death (which is only an elaboration of the emphasis we have already described) was thus spread widely. And the moral is the same as that in all the other literature: think of death, for only by such thought can your soul be saved.

Sic te in omni facto et cogitatu [says Thomas à Kempis] deberes habere: quasi hodie esses moriturus. . . . Beatus qui horam mortis suae semper ante oculos habet: et ad moriendum cotidie se disponit. Si vidisti aliquando hominem mori, cogita quia et tu per eandem viam transibis.[29]

5

Such, then, is the fourteenth-century emphasis on death. No wonder the subject weighed on people's

28. *Summa Praed.*, D. 11, 8–10, quoted by G. G. Coulton, *Five Centuries of Religion*, Cambridge, England, 1923, i, 169.

29. *De Imitatione Christi*, i, 23.

minds; "nam et multi metu moriendi moriuntur,"[30] Jacques de Vitry had said earlier, as if it were something everyone was aware of. But there was more to come; by the year 1400, this morbid attitude had not yet reached its climax.

For in spite of the fact that contemplation of death was urged by the Church, and the act of dying, even as early as Innocent III, was described as horrible beyond conception, the image of death presented either to the outer or inner eye, in art or literature, was not a particularly unpleasant one. The tomb figures of the thirteenth century are calm and peaceful; the English crusaders sleep in the Temple church quietly, and the kings and queens of France lie with all their regalia copied in marble at St. Denis. But at the end of the fourteenth century, death, in such monuments, suddenly becomes horrible. M. Mâle shows a picture of one of the first representations of this new aspect: the funeral monument of the Cardinal Lagrange (1402), now in the Musée Calvet at Avignon. His body is shown half-decomposed, a frightful warning to those who pass by; here, says M. Mâle, is that "réalisme funèbre dont les grands siècles du moyen âge n'eurent aucune idée." [31]

Once discovered, this new method of presentation had a tremendous appeal. It was, after all, a

---

30. Beeson, *Primer of Medieval Latin*, Chicago, 1925, p. 50.
31. Mâle, *op. cit.*, p. 348.

natural development. For the mystics and the
preachers and the poets had for almost a hundred
years been emphasizing, realistically and emotionally, the cruel aspects of Christ's death: the crown of
thorns, the shrunken flesh, the nails, the vinegar,
and the spear. What more natural than that art,
always pressing its emotionalism further and further
home, should exploit the horrible in the death of
ordinary individuals? It had been done already
in literature. There was the familiar reminder
"wormes fode thu schald beo," [32] repeated thou-
sands of times; and also more detailed descriptions:

> Nu schal for-rotien
>   thine teth and thi tunge.
> thi Mahe and thi Milte,
>   thi lyvre and thi lunge,
> And thi throte-bolle
>   that thu Mide sunge,
> And thu schalt in the putte.
>   faste beon ithrunge.[33]

---

32. "Long Life," v. 34 in *An Old English Miscellany*, ed. R.
Morris, E. E. T. S. (1872), p. 157.

33. "Death," in *Old English Misc.*, *ed. cit.*, pp. 169 ff., vv. 169 ff.
There is another fourteenth-century poem which paints the same
picture. Though a man sit like a king looking about him, says
the writer, to-morrow, who knows? He may be disgusting to all
his friends, wrapped about in a cloth, and

> "Hyse eres shullen dewen,
> And his eyen shallen dymen,
> And his nese shal sharpen,
> And his skyn shal starken,
> And his hew shal falewen,
> And his tonge shal stameren,
> And his lippes shulle quaken,

The physical characteristics, that is, both of the act of dying and of the body after death were described. This is significant, for it offers a striking contrast to the manner in which Innocent and the author of *The Pricke of Conscience* had described death. They had been concerned with its "spiritual" aspects: the recollection of past sins, the sight of ordinarily invisible devils. But these poems, and the statue of Cardinal Lagrange which had so many parallels, do nothing of the sort. They emphasize bodily decomposition only, not spiritual fear; they describe the fact, and leave the moral to be implied. Realism has outgrown its original position as subservient to emotion, and is used for its own sake. In other words, what seems to be a symptom of the decadence of the Middle Ages is in reality a further step to the Renaissance.

It is in this period, at the beginning of the fifteenth century, that the skeleton is for the first time universally accepted as the symbol of death. Previously there had been some uncertainty: in the frescoes in the Campo Santo at Pisa, Death is an old man with

---

> And his teth shulle ratelen,
> And his throte shal rotelen,
> And his feet shullen streken,
> And his herte shal breken."

(*Reliquiae Antiquae*, ed. T. Wright and J. O. Halliwell, London, 1845, 1, 64.) For a further discussion of poems on this subject see K. Brunner, "Mittelenglische Todesgeschichte," *Archiv für das Studium der Neueren Sprachen*, vol. 167 (1935), 19 ff.

a scythe flying through the air, and an English
fourteenth-century poem describes death as a
woman with hollow fiery eyes, lean cheeks,

> a marvelous mouth full of long tushes,
> & the neb of her nose to her navell hanged.[34]

But from the fifteenth century on there is no am-
biguity: the skeleton is everywhere. Why it should
have thus leapt into prominence is not easy to determine. The plague may have had some influence,
for from 1348, when it first made its appearance,
decomposing corpses were a very common sight, the
all too obvious indication of mortality. And there
seems to be some indication that the process was a
gradual one; the skeleton, in the monument of
Cardinal Lagrange and in the early Dance of Death
at La Chaise-Dieu in Auvergne, is at first covered
with decaying flesh; only later does it appear as the
bare articulated bone. But whatever its history may
be, the skeleton, once discovered, became unquestionably accepted, and to the present day no other
symbol of death has taken its place.

The best-known way in which the skeleton was
used in the fifteenth century was in the Dance of
Death — a phenomenon so curious and in its origins
so obscure, that a small library about it has col-

---

34. "Death and Life," vv. 168–169, *The Percy Folio MS.*, ed.
J. W. Hales and F. J. Furnivall, London, 1868, iii, 49 ff. The poem
was written shortly after 1380.

lected.[35] Everyone, I imagine, knows what a Dance of Death was like; a series of pictures painted on the walls of ecclesiastical buildings and elsewhere which showed how emperor and pope, empress and king, everyone down to the lowest peasant and the child "at his modiris brest sowkand," is led away by a dancing and grinning skeleton. The Dances of Death were nearly everywhere. Originating in France at the end of the fourteenth century, they soon became fashionable all over Europe; there was one at Paris, at Basle, Lubeck, Leipzig, Dresden, Nuremberg, Blois; at St. Paul's in London, at Stratford-on-Avon, at Bergamo, and Venice.[36] The spirit

35. The Dance of Death was not without its prototypes. The story of the Three Dead and the Three Living is chronologically earlier than the Dance itself, and both in meaning and popularity is its forerunner. The story is well known: three young men of high rank are suddenly confronted by three dead men; they draw back horrified; the dead speak, and the living retrace their steps. According to some authorities (Mâle, *op. cit.*, pp. 355 ff.; K. Künstle, *Die Legende der Drei Lebenden und der Drei Toten*, Frieburg, 1908), the legend begins in the thirteenth century, and it had an enormous popularity. In two versions (in one of which the young men are on foot, in the other, on horseback) it spread all over Europe — both in art and in literature. It was painted in the Campo Santo at Pisa (see Künstle, *op. cit.*, pl. VI), at the Innocents in Paris, in Normandy, Lorraine, etc.; it occurred in manuscripts and miniatures; and when printing came in, it was repeated in woodcuts. The verses (by Baudoin de Condé, Nicholas de Margival, and two anonymous poets, Mâle, *op. cit.*, p. 355) which described it were copied and re-copied throughout the fourteenth century.

36. See G. Buchheit, *Der Totentanz*, Berlin, 1926, and L. P. Kurtz, *The Dance of Death and The Macabre Spirit in European Literature*, New York, 1934.

of them all is shown in one of the earliest, that in the church at La Chaise-Dieu in Auvergne: grinning figures, with too much skin and sinew tightly covering them to be quite called skeletons, are each seizing a figure — a cardinal, a knight, a king — who resign themselves with a kind of melancholy desperation to their inevitable captors.[37] No one, is the obvious moral, can escape: death is the master of the world.

It has been frequently observed that the Dances of Death have very little about them that is Christian. Those grinning skeletons, tugging at their wretched victims with fiendish glee, playing on hornpipes, throwing their bony legs in the air with a wild kind of delight, do not reflect the quieter and more spiritual teaching of the Church. They fit in with it, of course, yet, unlike the earlier story of the Three Dead and the Three Living, they are somewhat aside from the main current of ecclesiastical teaching. But they are in the very center of the other currents of their time. They are a natural outgrowth of the realistic technique the late Middle Ages so increasingly emphasized; and the sentiment they express — that death levels everything — is one which the rising bourgeois class could contemplate with considerable pleasure. As Miss Hammond remarks, "The bourgeois spectator of the

37. W. Stammler, *Die Totentanze des Mittelalters*, Munich, 1922, pl. 1.

Dance shared the harsh satisfaction of Death himself in levelling social differences. In such and similar insistences on the fragility of human prosperity, the spirit of the time revelled." [38]

But there were, besides these examples of gay morbidity, of life in death, other representations of death's triumph. At Bergamo he is a crowned skeleton, covered with a rich mantle, who stands on a tomb with his bony arms outstretched over a crowd of kings and great men who kneel before him offering him rich gifts in vain.[39] Perhaps most striking of all are the triumphs of death painted by Peter Breughel the elder in the early sixteenth century. Here there is no single skeleton king, but a host of conquering skeletons, who drive everyone before them in a kind of frenzied exaltation.

It is hardly an exaggeration to say that in Northern Europe the whole fifteenth century was frenzied about death. The *Ars Moriendi* was one of the first examples of printing, and it had appeared everywhere before the fifteenth century expired. A great poet, like Villon, had nothing but death to write about; the form of the "testament" was the only literary form in his day that was, paradoxically, alive. The emphasis on death seems to have mounted like a rushing tide. All the teaching in

38. *English Verse between Chaucer and Surrey*, Durham, North Carolina, 1927, p. 130. E. Döring-Hirsch, *Tod und Jenseits im Spätmittelalter*, Berlin, 1927, also emphasizes this point.

39. Reproduced in Künstle, *op. cit.*, pl. IV.

connection with it which prevailed in the century before, was repeated with additional emphasis; the skeleton became more and more prevalent; one can hardly pick up a poem or look at a picture of that time in which his figure does not appear. The fourteenth century, dismal as it may seem, was only the beginning of this morbid emphasis. Not until the fifteenth did death's ghastly symbol become universally recognized. And how common it was, how even fashionable it had grown, may be exemplified by a poem written about 1500 (the date is uncertain) by "Skelton Lauriat, uppon a deedmans hed, that was sent to hym from an honorable jentyllwoman for a token." Skelton, on receiving such an emblem of friendship, "devysd this gostly medytacyon in English, convenable, in sentence comendable, lamentable, lacrymable, profytable for the soule":

Youre ugly tokyn	From Deth holow-eyed,
My mynd hath brokyn	With synnews wyderyd,
From worldly lust;	With bonys shyderyd,
For I have dyscust	With hys worme-etyn maw,
We ar but dust,	And his gastly jaw
And dy we must. . . .	Gaspying asyde,
I have well espyde	Nakyd of hyde,
No man may hym hyde	Neyther flesh nor fell.[40]

Skelton's moral is the old moral of a thousand other poems; we all must die — "mynes vous y"

40. Poems of Skelton, ed. R. Hughes, London, 1924, p. 62.

— and if you do remember, the Virgin, in return, will preserve you from the fiends. And just as the sentiment is conventional (so conventional that one does not take Skelton very seriously when he repeats it), so is the description of death itself; it is the same hollow-eyed spectre that danced, with a rattle of its reminding bones, through the grey atmosphere of the dying Middle Ages.

Chapter II

THE SIXTEENTH–CENTURY CONFLICT

"My God's my arm; my life my heaven, my grave
To me all end."

Marston, *Sophonisba*

"We must always look to this end, to use ourselves to the
contempt of this present life, and thereby be stirred to the
meditation of the life to come."

Calvin, *Institutes of the Christian Religion*

I

IT WOULD be foolish to suppose, because death
and the skeleton were so heavily emphasized
in the late Middle Ages, that men had no other interests; on the contrary, the message of the skeleton
was perhaps vividly emphasized just because those
opposing interests were so strong. At any rate a conflict was inevitable; even in the most tired of civiliza-
tions human nature is bound to recoil from continual
contemplation of death and another world. And
the late fifteenth century in Northern Europe was by
no means tired — it was full of a tumultuous life.
New currents of thought were sweeping up from the
South; the period shook with a violent, if confused,
energy; and the very fact that its emphasis on death
took so exuberant a form as that of the Dances,
shows that the spirit of the time was not prepared to

accept the orthodox teaching with a bowed head and lowered eyes. Men thought of material things as much as they always have, and there were few individuals who were restrained from trying to impress their neighbors with external magnificence by the thought that their glory was only food for worms.

As the sixteenth century began, and the worldly ideals of Italy spread more widely through France and England, the emphasis on the present life naturally increased, and one would expect to find that the old teaching about death had correspondingly begun to fade. But this was not so. The more joyous the voice of life grew, the louder became the hollow tones of death, and beneath all the grandeur of the Field of the Cloth of Gold men still saw the mockery of the skull.

It is this conflict between the interests of the present world and those of the next which makes the sixteenth century — and the Elizabethan drama which was its later product — so fascinating. To be sure, the conflict seems much clearer to us, as we look back on it, than it did to the people of the sixteenth century themselves — to them it was largely unconscious; Holbein doubtless saw nothing but propriety in the fact that having painted the magnificent dress of his ambassadors, he should put a skull at their feet.[1] Life and the reminders of death were

1. The fashion of including skulls in portraits lasted well into the seventeenth century. For example, the "Portrait of a Gentle-

closely united, and to know that death was always in the background gave to the incidents of life a zeal and color which they might otherwise have lacked. Even when the awareness of the conflict between the two values was blurred, its subterraneous presence added intensity to thought and energy to passion.

But the conflict was not always unconscious: it had, in fact, been very clearly articulated by a man of remarkable sensibility a hundred and fifty years before the sixteenth century began. Not without reason has Petrarch been called "the first of the moderns," and in no way does he more clearly show his modernity than in his awareness of the clash between the two values I have mentioned. His *Secretum*, or *De Contemptu Mundi*, or *De Conflictu Curarum Suarum*, as it is variously called, is for our purposes one of the most important documents of the Renaissance, and it will be well worth while to examine it briefly before we proceed to discuss the immediate background of the drama, for no other work describes so clearly the elements of which that background was composed.

The book, which was written between 1342 and 1353, consists of a three days' dialogue between Petrarch and St. Augustine on the relative merits of

---

man," by Nason, in the Dulwich Gallery, shows a skull on the table in the lower right-hand corner. This picture dates from the early years of the Restoration.

a life spent in pursuing earthly things — love, literature, and fame — and a life spent in preparation
for death and the rewards of the world to come.[2]
St. Augustine of course upholds the latter opinion,
and he puts forth, with all the literary skill that
Petrarch was able to give him, those arguments with
which we are already familiar, but which had rarely
before been expressed so well.

There can be no doubt [he begins] that to recollect one's
misery and to practice frequent meditation on death is the
surest aid in scorning the seductions of this world, and in or-
dering the soul amid its storms and tempests, if only such meditation be not superficial, but sink into the bones and marrow
of the heart. . . . We must picture to ourselves the effect of
death on each several part of our bodily frame, the cold ex-
tremities, the breast in the sweat of fever, the side throbbing
with pain, the vital spirits running slower and slower as death
draws near, the eyes sunken and weeping, every look filled
with tears, the forehead pale and drawn, the cheeks hanging
and hollow, the teeth staring and discolored, the nostrils shrunk
and sharpened, the lips foaming, the tongue foul and motion-
less. . . . This, then, is what I meant by sinking down deeply
into the soul.[3]

Such meditation, St. Augustine goes on to say, is
all to no purpose unless it has a violent result:

If in the act of meditation you find yourself suddenly grow
stiff, if you tremble, turn pale, and feel as if already you endured its pains; if at the same time you seem to yourself as

---

2. English translation by W. H. Draper, London, 1911. An
excellent analysis of its contents is to be found in J. H. Robinson
and H. W. Rolfe, *Petrarch*, New York, 1914, pp. 413 ff.

3. First dialogue, Draper's trans., pp. 7, 32–33.

if you were leaving your body behind, and were forced to render up your account before the bar of eternal judgment . . . if you realize . . . that death itself will not turn aside for any plea; that it is not the end of sufferings, but only a passage: if you picture to yourself a thousand forms of punishment and pain, the noise and wailing of Hell, the sulphurous rivers, the thick darkness, and avenging Furies, — in a word, the fierce malignity everywhere of that dark abode; and, what is the climax of its horror, that the misery knows no end, and despair thereof itself is everlasting, since the time of God's mercy is passed by; if, I say, all these things rise up before your eyes at once, not as fictions but as truth, not as being possible, but inevitable, and of a surety bound to come, yes, and even now at the door . . . then you may be assured you have not meditated in vain.[4]

There is much more to the same effect, and if St. Augustine's listener had been anyone save Petrarch, his conversion would have followed immediately. But Petrarch, at the end of the long argument, refuses to submit. He agrees that Augustine is right, yet in spite of everything, he will not, as Augustine advises, surrender his literary studies or his pursuit of earthly fame for the sake of an other-worldly ideal. "Such glory as belongs to man is enough for me. That is all I sigh after. Mortal myself, it is but mortal blessings I desire." [5] And, he continues,

there is a certain justification for my plan of life. It may be only glory that we seek here, but I persuade myself that, as long as we remain here, that is right. Another glory awaits us

---

4. *Ibid.*, pp. 34–35.
5. Third dialogue, Draper, p. 172.

in heaven and he who reaches there will not wish even to think of earthly fame. So this is the natural order, that among mortals the care of things mortal should come first; to the transitory will then succeed the eternal; from the first to the second is the natural progression.[6]

This is an extremely interesting conclusion, and it is filled with important implications. For Petrarch is the first man, not to make the conflict between this world and the next explicit — that had been done countless times before — but to decide the issue in favor of earthly things. For the first time under Christianity, human interests are seriously admitted to be valuable for their own sakes, and earthly glory worthy of man's best endeavor. It is for this reason that we may call the *Secretum* the first document in the history of the modern mind.

2

We do not find, for many years, another explicit statement like this. The convention which emphasized the other world was too strong, and few people were as self-conscious in analyzing their feelings as was Petrarch. Nevertheless the curiosity about the external world, the interest in human relationships and the passion for fame which Petrarch did his best to maintain, became steadily stronger, particularly in Italy, after his death. The influence of these things was insidious, for they were at first expressed

6. Third dialogue, trans. in Robinson and Rolfe, *op. cit.*, p. 452.

as part of religion, just as the realism with which they were described had first been encouraged as an aid to the contemplation of the Passion of Christ.

For example, in Italian and Flemish sacred pictures of the fifteenth century, we begin to find a kneeling figure in the corner, the donor of the picture, whose presence there shows that he wanted it known by whom the work was given.[7] Fra Angelico, the most devout of all Renaissance artists, began his career with over-delicate and pretty little pictures of pink and blue angels crowning a doll-like Virgin in a golden heaven; in his second period, his figures became life-sized and dignified, standing by themselves in gardens among rocks; he ended by painting scenes from the life of St. Laurence in a thoroughly realistic fashion. And in Flanders before the year 1500, portrait painting was already a highly developed art.

These facts are of course familiar, and it would be easy to add to them, but it will clarify our discussion of the Elizabethan background if we limit ourselves to the terms of Petrarch's discussion. For just as fifteenth-century painting asserted the value of the

7. In Fra Lippo Lippi's "Coronation of the Virgin," the kneeling figure is the painter himself. In the magnificent Avignon "Pietà" in the Louvre (*circa* 1425), the kneeling donor seems to be painted in a more realistic style than the other figures, as if he were a contemporary, transplanted by a feat of historical imagination into events belonging to the past. This is even more striking in a less familiar painting of the same school, the "Adoration" in the Musée Calvet at Avignon.

individual — the realism which had first been the
handmaid of religion breaking away to freedom,
and expressing, untrammeled, its sense of delight
in the external world — so in literature and in life
we find a growing sense of the individual's value
and, following Petrarch, an assertion of his right to
fame.

Petrarch had himself written a poem called *The
Triumph of Fame*, a rather pedantic work consisting
of a long list of largely classical figures who by the
excellence of their deeds had established a reputation which could conquer death. He advised his
ideal prince to cherish scholars so that he would be
remembered by future generations,[8] and in his
Epistle to Posterity he attempted, by writing about
himself, to make, in his own case, such scholars unnecessary. Chaucer's *Hous of Fame* shows an interest, if not a personal one, in the subject; and though
Northern European literature in the fifteenth century did little to develop the tradition, in Italy fame
was pursued with an almost morbid enthusiasm.
"Courage, Girolamo!" cried one of the murderers
of Galeazzo Sforza, as the executioner was breaking
his ribs, "Thou wilt long be remembered; death is
bitter, but glory is eternal!" [9] Several fifteenth-

8. *Epistolae Senilis*, lib. xiv, 1; quoted in J. Burckhardt, *Civilization of the Renaissance in Italy*, Eng. trans., London, 1898, pp. 9–10.
For the Italian emphasis on fame in general see Burckhardt,
part 2, ch. 3.

9. Buckhardt, *op. cit.*, p. 58.

century Italians were willing to commit any kind of villainy if it would make them famous, and most of the humanists managed to convince both themselves and their patrons that immortality was to be conferred by praise given in their writings.[10] Aretino affords the best-known example of this, but he was only one among many. Francesco Filelfo, for instance, "perfected the business of immortalizing into a formal system. Firmly convinced of the immortality of his Latin letters and verse, he thought no less confidently that a praising or blaming mention in them would be the standard for the judgment of posterity." [11]

Such extravagances were not common in England, but echoes of the Italian convention in a milder form were frequent enough in the sixteenth century, particularly in the elegies and epitaphs which were rapidly becoming fashionable. Sir David Lyndsay ends his poem on the death of Queen Magdalene of Scotland (1537) by saying that her fame shall have victory over death,[12] and somewhat later (*circa* 1546), when writing his "Testament of Squyer Meldrum," he makes his hero say:

> My time is gane, I think it bot ane dreame,
> Yit efter deith romane sall my gude fame.[13]

---

10. *Ibid.*, pp. 151–153.
11. G. Voigt, *Die Wiederbelebung des Classischen Alterthums*, Berlin, 1893, I, 527.
12. *Works*, ed. G. Chalmers, London, 1806, II, 188.
13. *Ibid.*, II, 308.

With Turberville (whose *Epitaphes*, etc., appeared in
1567: "A fewe Sonets, the unripe seedes of my bar-
raine braine, to pleasure and recreate thy wearye
mind and troubled hed withal"), the very fact that
a man dies at all seems to ensure him a lasting fame.
In his "Funerall Verse upon the Death of Sir John
Horsey, knight," he remarks:

> For Horsey gaines by death's outragious spight,
> An endlesse fame, whereat his foes repine.[14]

And in seven other of his "Epitaphes," Turberville
uses this same idea of the immortality of fame.
Death cannot get the conquest of fame, says George
Whetstone, in 1585,[15] having already made the remark that a virtuous life cannot be destroyed by
death.[16] Anthony Copley, in *A Fig for Fortune* (1596),
went even further:

> Thy Spirrit is a particle of *Jove* . . .
> And take but Glory from it, and it dies:
> > Yet dies it not, but to indignitie,
> > Mounting by Death, to Fames eternitie.[17]

One can see from these examples how generally
the notion was accepted, and how it grew as the six-

14. *Epitaphes, Epigrams, Songs and Sonets*, ed. J. P. Collier (n. d.),
p. 135.

15. "The Life, death, and devine virtues of . . . Frauncis
Earle of Bedford," printed in *Heliconia*, ed. T. Park, London, 1815,
vol. II.

16. *The Rocke of Regarde*, ed. J. P. Collier (n. d.), "An epitaphe
upon . . . Henry Cantrell," p. 230.

17. Ed. Spenserian Society, London, 1883, p. 5.

teenth century progressed. Perhaps the best statement of it is to be found in the dedicatory epistle to
the 1587 edition of the *Mirror for Magistrates*: the
writer there speaks of "desire of fame, glorye, re-
nowne, and immortalitie (to which all men well
nighe by nature are inclined, especially those which
excell or have any singuler gift of fortune or the
body)." [18] *The Mirror for Magistrates*, with its long
and dreary accounts of the falls of princes, is, be it
remembered, a book with a medieval subject, but
the remark just quoted would never have prefaced
such a volume in the Middle Ages.

A little later we find the more definitely Italian
convention of the sonneteers that by the poet's
praise, the subject of his poem will achieve undying
fame. The Italians had taken this convention from
Latin poetry, where it is common. Several Roman
poets had also spoken confidently of the enduring
fame their art would bring them; the Renaissance
was doubtless best acquainted with the "monu-
mentum aere perennius" of Horace, and the equally
well-known lines at the end of Ovid's *Metamor-
phoses*:

> Iamque opus exegi, quod nec Iovis ira nec ignes
> Nec poterit ferrum nec adax abolere vetustas.
> Cum volet, illa dies, quae nil nisi corporis huius
> Ius habet, incerti spatium mihi finiat aevi:
> Parte tamen meliore mei super alta perennis
> Astra ferar, nomenque erit indelebile nostrum.

---

18. Ed. J. Haslewood, London, 1815, I, 4.

The sentiment is familiar to all readers of Elizabethan literature. Besides Shakespeare's famous
sonnet (xviii), ending:

> So long as men can breathe, or eyes can see,
> So long lives this, and this gives life to thee,

and Christopher Brooke's lines on Prince Henry:

> And tho this phoenix (fled from any ken)
> Have sacrificed his life in funerall flame,
> A Poet's magicke yet prevailes in death;
> Adds life to vertue and gives honor breath — [19]

besides these, there were almost countless other expressions of the same thing, in sonnets, dedications,
and the like, throughout the reigns of Elizabeth and
James. It is unnecessary to quote further examples;
it is already clear that by 1600 the opinion most opposed to late medieval teaching had become thoroughly accepted as a literary convention — possibly
as an article of actual belief.

3

Anxiety to keep one's name remembered after
death has, of course, always been recognized as an
element in human nature. "Omnibus fere ingenita
est famae post mortem cupido," said Tertullian; [20]
but unlike the dedicator of the *Mirror for Magis-*

19. "Poems of Christopher Brooke," in *Miscellanies of the Fuller
Worthies' Library*, ed. A. B. Grosart, London, 1871, IV, 178 (1614).
20. "De Testimonio Animae," Migne, *Pat. Lat.*, I, col. 615.

trates, he added that such a desire, since it was unworthy of a good Christian, must be vigorously subdued.

And all orthodox opinion in the sixteenth century agreed with him. In spite of the growing passion for fame, and the increasingly widespread interest in the things of this world which the period obviously showed, the emphasis on the vileness of man and the importance of death which the fifteenth century had brought to such a feverish pitch was in no way checked by the imaginary barrier of the year 1500. On the contrary, the temperature rose, and there seemed little prospect of its settling back to normal. Calvinism, for one thing, took the teaching over entire; the founders of the new Christianity recognized that one of their strongest means of securing proselytes was to direct into new channels the tradition they found already established. "With whatsoever kinde of trouble we be distressed [writes Calvin], we must alway looke to this end, to use our selves to the contempt of this present life, and thereby be stirred to the meditation of the life to come." [21] And again:

If we must live and die to the Lord, let us leave to his will the time of our life and death; but so that wee bee still fervent in desire of death, and be continually occupied in meditation

---

21. *Institutes of Christian Religion*, III, chap. 9, sec. 1, tr. T. Norton, London, 1634.

thereof, and despise this life in comparison of the immortalitie to come, and wish to forsake it when it shall please the Lord, because of the bondage of sinne.[22]

The familiar doctrine could not have been put more concisely. And it was, of course, continually repeated in England. Thomas Becon, in his very popular work, *The Sick Man's Salve* (1561), remarks: "certes our mortal estate declareth evidently, that we be so bond unto death, that we are not certain of our life one hour." [23] Man, says Latimer in his first "Sermon on the Card," "is the child of the ire and indignation of God, the true inheritor of hell, a lump of sin, and working nothing of (himself) but all towards hell." Becon, in his "Prayer for the Health of the Body," says, "I feel in myself . . . how grievous a prison this my body is unto my soul, which continually wisheth to be loosened out of this vile carcase." [24] The contemplation of death alone could make life secure. Francis Quarles only echoed the sixteenth century in saying:

> If I must die, I'll snatch at every thing
> That may but mind me of my latest breath;
> Death's-heads, graves, knells, blacks,
> Tombs. . . .[25]

---

22. *Ibid.*, III, chap. 9, sec. 4.

23. *The Sick Man's Salve, Prayers and Other Pieces*, ed. J. Ayre, Cambridge, England, 1844. This work went through numerous editions, and several references to it are to be found in the dramatists.

24. "Pomander of Prayer," *ed. cit.*, p. 83.

25. Francis Quarles, quoted by F. P. Weber, *Aspects of Death*, London, 1918, p. 135.

Early sixteenth-century drama, often virtually a part of religion, made much of death. As a person, death had only appeared once in the earlier mystery plays: the Coventry play, the "Death of Herod," describes *Mors* entering —

> I am deth goddys masangere —

to seize the king's soul.[26] But in the first decades of the sixteenth century there are between twenty and thirty German plays which include death as an actor,[27] and many English moralities base their plots on the fact that death is the end of all things, and that life is to be regulated accordingly. *Everyman* is the best known of these, but *Pride of Life* and *The Castle of Perseverance* are built on the same lines. Death here performs a double role: from one point of view he is the voice of God — "goddys masangere" — as in *Everyman*; from another he is the ally of the devils, and gives them their expected prey.[28]

The art of the period literally teems with pictures of death. Holbein seems to have been particularly fond of the subject, for he designed a Dance of

26. *Ludus Coventriae*, ed. K. S. Block, London, 1922, pp. 174 ff.

27. I owe this information to the kindness of Mr. J. Vander-heyden, who has studied the treatment of death in the Low Countries during the Middle Ages and the Renaissance. In his opinion the height of the emphasis on death in that district was during the 'thirties of the sixteenth century.

28. On this point see R. L. Ramsay's excellent introduction to his edition of Skelton's *Magnyficence*, E. E. T. S. (1906), pp. xliii, clxxvi.

Death for the sheath of a dagger; [29] he painted portraits in which a grinning skeleton, holding a scythe,
lurks in the background; [30] he designed an alphabet
of death; and he painted a *danse macabre*, we are told,
in the palace of Whitehall.[31] More important than
any of these is his well-known series of woodcuts,
first printed at Lyons in 1538: *Les Simulachres et His-
toriees Faces de la Mort, autant Elegamment Pourtraictes,
que Artificiellement Imaginees.* The pictures are much
the same (only far more skilfully executed) as those
in the older Dances of Death; their moral, and the
moral of the verses which accompany them, is the
old one we have so often heard:

> Si tu veulx vivre sans peché
> Voy ceste image a tous propos,
> Et point ne seras empeché
> Quand tu t'en iras a rêpos.[32]

A series of similar pictures was included in what
has been called "Queen Elizabeth's Prayer Book"
— *A book of Christian Prayers, collected out of the An-
cient writers*, etc., first published at London in 1569.
This was reprinted in 1578, 1581, 1590, and 1609.
And there were many more such drawings on the
Continent, particularly in Germany, all "for the

29. Reproduced in Weber, *op. cit.*, p. 707.

30. *Ibid.*, p. 133.

31. See F. Douce, *Holbein's Dance of Death*, London, 1858, pp.
124 ff. The Whitehall palace was destroyed by fire in 1697.

32. This work was extremely popular; it went through ten
editions in twenty-six years, chiefly in France and Germany.

good of the souls of the well-inclined readers to
awaken in them a lively fear and diligent anticipa-
tion of death."

Up to 1550, the emphasis on death became more
and more universal, and at times even diseased.
From the first half of the sixteenth century date
these church statues of partly decomposed corpses,
which are not funeral monuments, as such things
had been a hundred years before, but merely warn-
ings: "Such as I am, so will you be." [33] Some of the
German pictures of the time, showing heads and
bodies with all the details of corruption, are horrible
— so disgusting that one can hardly bear to look at
them.[34] The warning was everywhere. There were
houses in Brittany and Scotland with *memento mori*
carved on them; winepots were inscribed with
verses:

Pense a la mort, povre sot; [35]

ambassadors, fashionable ladies, Dr. Martin Luther,
Puritans and whores, all wore *memento mori* jewelry
on their persons,[36] and in George Gascoigne's Eng-

33. Mâle, *L'Art Religieux de la Fin du Moyen Age en France*, Paris,
1925, p. 350.

34. See Weber, *op. cit.*, p. 433, where one of these monstrosities
is reproduced.

35. Mâle, *op. cit.*, pp. 352–353; Weber, *op. cit.*, p. 691. The
Edinburgh houses are still visible.

36. See Weber, *op. cit., passim.* In Holbein's picture, "The Am-
bassador," in the National Gallery, Jean de Dinteville, Lord of
Polisy, is represented wearing a *memento mori* jewel (a death's-head
of silver or white enamel set in gold) as a cap-piece. A lady named

lish garden there was a chair on which could be
read the following typical lines:

If thou sitte here to viewe this pleasant garden place,
Think thus; at last will come a frost, and al these flowers deface.
But if thou sitte at ease to rest thy weary bones,
Remember death brings finall rest to all oure grevous grones.
So whether for delyght, or here thou sitte for ease,
Think stille upon the latter day, so shalt thou God best please.[37]

All serious opinion, public and private, Roman
Catholic and Protestant, said the same thing:
"Memento homo quod cinis es!" "Cogita mori ut
vivas!" — the warning was shouted from all points
of the compass. Think of death, for the whole
race of Adam is corrupt with sin, and only by
thinking of death may the stain be removed.

Agnes Hals, in a will dated 1554, bequeathed to her niece her gold
ring "with the weping eie," and to her son her ring "with the
dead manes head. . . ." Dr. Martin Luther is said to have worn
a gold finger-ring with the words "Mori saepe cogita!" (Weber,
op. cit., p. 692). On p. 693 Weber gives a picture of one of these
rings, and on p. 697 a list of the mottoes engraved on them —
"Remember death," "Live to die," etc. Marston speaks of the
whores' use of the fashion in *The Dutch Courtezan*: "As for their
[loose women's] death, how can it be bad, since their wickedness is
always before their eyes, and a death's-head most commonly upon
their middle finger?" In Massinger's *Old Law* is a similar passage: "Sell some of thy cloaths to buy thee a death's-head, and
put upon thy middle finger. Your least considering bawds do so
much" (quoted by Weber, p. 694). There is some characteristic
memento mori jewelry in the Musée de Cluny, at Paris.

37. *A Hundreth Sundrie Flowers* (1573), ed. B. M. Ward, London,
1926, p. 139.

4

Such, described as briefly as possible, are the two sides of the picture. On the one hand, the present world, the value of the individual and his right to fame are considered increasingly important; on the other, man's sin, the vanity of worldly life and the imminence of death are to be contemplated with the greatest possible intensity. Though the emphasis on death did not increase after reaching its climax shortly before the middle of the century, it can hardly be said to have suffered a decline, and as the convention of fame became widespread toward the end of the period, the necessity of contemplating death remained in the background as a part of the universally accepted doctrine. In 1554 the courtier John Haryngton, when confined with the princess Elizabeth in the Tower, wrote a set of very orthodox verses in which he remarked:

> Death is a porte whereby we pass to joye;
>   Lyfe is a lake that drownethe all in payne;
> Death is so dear, it killeth all annoye;
>   Lyfe is so lewd, that all it yields is vayne.[38]

The lines show how easily, how almost automatically, the thought sprang to mind.

38. *Nugae Antiquae*, ed. H. Harington and T. Park, London, 1804, II, 333. This poem was popular and was reprinted in several of the later anthologies.

But there was soon to be a change. In 1557 *Tottel's Miscellany* appeared, and for the first time in England the two opposing views of life were stated side by side. For though Wyatt and Surrey, the two chief contributors, say nothing directly about fame or the delights of worldly glory, the fact that the great majority of their poems is concerned with love, and expresses strong personal emotion about earthly objects, is of great significance. The poems may derive from Petrarch, but the Petrarchan influence rather adds to, than detracts from, their historical value. Poetry is no longer a vehicle for story-telling, for allegorical moralities or simplified history; it is used for expressing directly the feelings of one human being for another.

Yet the poems in this volume are by no means only of this world. "A Comparison of Life and Death" [39] comes to the conclusion that

> If man would minde, what burdens life doth bring . . .
> He would sure think, as with great cause I do:
> The day of death were better of the two. . . .
> Wherfore with Paul let all men wish, and pray
> To be dissolvde of this foule fleshy masse.[40]

Such statements are common throughout the book; they occur again and again in the later anthologies:

39. *Tottel's Miscellany*, ed. H. E. Rollins, Cambridge, Massachusetts, 1928, I, 125.

40. See also the epitaph on W. Chambers, p. 109, and "Upon consideracion of the state of this lyfe he wisheth death," p. 127, which say the same thing.

> And what is manne — dust, slime, a puffe of winde,
> Conceavde in sinne, plaste in the world with greefe,
> Brought up with care, till care hath caught his minde,
> And then till death vouchsafe him some releefe . . .

says one of the contributors to the *Paradise of Dainty Devices*.[41] This whole collection, like the *Gorgeous Gallery of Gallant Inventions* (1578), breathes a spirit of gloom. One of its first poems is called "Our Pleasures Are Vanities," through which runs an acrostic saying, in part: "Have mind on death and fear to sin," and we continually find titles like "Respice finem," "Finding worldly joyes but vanities he wisheth death," and "Thinke to Dye."

Countless such poems can be found after the middle of the sixteenth century, and it is unnecessary to quote them here.[42] They are not, after all, very serious expressions of opinion; they are rather the consequence of a moment's depression — "a dolorous verse, written by him, that indeede was in no small dumpes when he wrote them."[43] And the author

41. Ed. H. E. Rollins, Cambridge, Massachusetts, 1927, p. 120.

42. The reader may be referred to *The Mirror for Magistrates*, ed. J. Haslewood, London, 1815, "Lord Irenglas," stanza 10; Whetstone, *Rocke of Regarde* (1576), ed. J. P. Collier, London, n. d., p. 318; *Paradise of Dainty Devices*, and *Gorgeous Gallery of Gallant Inventions*, *passim*; Humphrey Gifford, "Posie of Gillowflowers" (1580), ed. A. B. Grosart, London, 1871; *Miscellanies of the Fuller Worthies Library*, I, 340; Henry Lok, *"Poems"* (1593–97), ed. Grosart, *Miscellanies*, II, 61 ff.; Timothe Kendall, *Flowers of Epigrammes* (1577), ed. Spenser Society (1874), p. 124.

43. A "Flourish upon Fancie" (1582), by Nicholas Breton, ed. T. Park, *Heliconia*, London, 1815, I, 124.

who was "in no small dumpes" one day, and expressed himself, while in them, after the medieval convention, would, on another occasion, advertise his work with a semi-humorous conceit that is not medieval at all: "A Flourish upon Fancie: as gallant a glose, upon so trifling a text, as ever was written." The two worlds, this and the next, are inextricably bound together; now one is evident, now the other, dependent on the mood that is uppermost; the opposing views exist side by side, apparently as unrelated as the two conflicting quotations I have put at the head of this chapter. A collection like *A Hundreth Sundrie Flowers* (1573)[44] is typical; most of the poems (Gascoigne is the author of the greater part of them) are concerned with love, and do not repeat the *memento mori* directions that are so frequent, for example, in the *Paradise of Dainty Devices*. But no collection of middle sixteenth-century verse could avoid such directions entirely. It is in this same collection that we find those gloomy verses which Gascoigne engraved on his garden chair. And there is a poem called "Gascoigne's Good-nyghte" which, in opposition to the general tone of the collection, is very medieval indeed.[45]

44. *Ed. cit.*
45. P. 109:
"The streking armes, the yawning breath, which I to bedward use,
    Are patternes of the pangs of deth, when lyfe will me refuse;

Yet after the 'seventies, these sentiments become more and more rare. *The Phoenix Nest* (1593)[46] may contain melancholy verses, but the melancholy springs from disappointment in love, not from a consideration of man's general wretchedness; *England's Helicon* (1600) [47] has nothing but love poems in it, and Campion's *Book of Airs* (1601)[48] does not men-

---

And of my bed eche sundrie parte in shadowes doth resemble
The sundry shapes of deth, whose dart shal make my flesh to
    tremble,
My bed itselfe is lyke the grave, my sheets the winding sheets,
My clothes the moulde which I must have to cover me most meet;
The hungry fleas which friske so fresh to worms I can compare,
Which greedily shal gnaw my flesh, and leave the bones ful bare,
    etc."

Gascoigne is compounded of two worlds. In May, 1572, a petition against him which prevented his taking his seat in Parliament included the following passage: "Item he is a notorious Ruffianne and especiallie noted to be bothe a Spie, an Atheist and Godles personne." His career was certainly a worldly one. But in 1576 he printed a work called *The Droomme of Doomesday* which is, in part, a translation from Innocent III's *De Contemptu Mundi*, than which nothing, as we know, can be more medieval. See *Cambridge History of English Literature*, III, 203, 208.

46. Ed. T. Park, *Heliconia*, London, 1815, vol. II.

47. Ed. Sir S. E. Brydges and J. Haslewood, London, 1812.

48. Ed. A. H. Bullen, *Works of Campion*, London, 1889. Campion's "Divine and Morall Poems," printed in 1613 but "long since composed," are quite different from works of a similar kind written a hundred years earlier. We find none of that *respice finem* attitude that was previously enforced by such grisly methods; they are personal lyrics only, and though earthly joys are said to be not comparable to heavenly ones, and man is by no means a perfect creature, nevertheless the moral is not the old one, and neither death nor the world the horrible things they formerly were.

tion death at all. The subject had apparently gone
out of fashion, and occupied a smaller place in
men's minds.

And if we look outside of literature, as we must if
our perspective is to be a true one, it is plain enough
that at the time when the drama was beginning its
intense career, the cause of the present world had
gained immensely. The court of Elizabeth in the
'eighties was full of vigor; ambition and jealousy,
intrigue and magnificence, adventure and lust,
swirled richly around the palace at Whitehall, or
followed the Queen as she moved grandly from one
lavish entertainment to another. The clothes on the
back of the courtier, in Nashe's words, bandied
"colours with the Sunne." "Nothing he talks on
but kentalls of Pearle, the conquering of *India*, and
fishing for Kingdomes." [49] Spenser wrote his great
work primarily "to fashion a gentleman," not, as an
earlier writer would have done, to fashion a Christian; and even Calvinism added greatly to the emphasis on the present world. It made the individual
more important than he had been before, and by its
concentration on faith rather than works, it made
religion a special thing apart; one's salvation had
already been predetermined by God, and provided
one had faith, and went to church on Sundays, one
could quite securely spend one's life in the pursuit

49. Nashe, "Christs Teares over Jerusalem," in *Works*, ed.
R. B. McKerrow, London, 1910, II, 81.

of prosperity and success.[50] Certainly success, and
the riches it implied, was sought everywhere, in
America, on the high seas, in India, and at home.
If we look only at the surface, the scorn of man's
natural abilities, the emphasis on death as the key
to true life, seem, at least by 1590, almost entirely to
have disappeared; the teaching of Petrarch's St. Augustine and the countless horde of his imitators —

> si lunga tratta
> di gente, ch'io non avrai mai creduto,
> che morte tanta n'avesse disfatta —

has apparently been erased from men's minds.

We can perhaps be led to discover whether or not
this is true by examining the *Essays* of Montaigne.
Montaigne, like Petrarch, knew what he thought, and
also had sufficient respect for the conventions of his
time not to offend propriety by openly attacking
them; in him there is an expression of both personal
and general opinion which will be very revealing
for our purpose. His earliest essay on the subject,
"That to philosophize is to learn to die" (I, 20),[51]
is indeed worth careful study, for it is the most interesting example I am acquainted with of the
marriage between the late medieval emphasis on
death and the sentiments on the subject which were
encouraged by the classics, and which were begin-

50. This point is well brought out by J. H. Randall, Jr., *The
Making of the Modern Mind*, Boston, 1926, p. 138.
51. *Essays*, trans. E. J. Trechmann, Oxford, 1927.

ning to be more and more sympathetic to the men
of the Renaissance. "Ever since I can remember,"
he says, "nothing has occupied my imagination
more than death, yea, even in the most licentious
season of my life." At dances, while playing games,
he used to fall into fits of abstraction, meditating on
those who, unsuspecting, had recently gone from
similar pastimes to a sudden end. And such meditation is to be commended. "Let us disarm him
[death] of his strangeness, let us bring him before
our imagination in his every shape. There is no evil
in life for him who has rightly understood that priva-
tion of life is no evil."

Such remarks are, of course, largely medieval,
with a mixture of Stoicism. But the conclusion to be
drawn from them has nothing medieval about it.
We are to contemplate death not, as the Church
would insist, that we may fear it, and order our lives
accordingly, but that we may become so inured to
its presence that we are unaffected by it. "I agree
that we should work and prolong the functions of
life as far as we can, and hope that Death may
find me planting my cabbages, but indifferent to
him and still more to the unfinished state of my
garden." [52]

52. For similar remarks, see bk. II, 13: "It [death] is indeed a meat that must be swallowed without chewing by one
whose throat is not lined with paving stones. . . . Caesar, when
asked what death he thought the most desirable, replied, 'the least
premeditated and the quickest.' If Caesar had the courage to say

Now this is a desire entirely contrary to that of a good churchman, who prayed, as he was taught, to be delivered from "sudden death." Bromyard, for example, would have been shocked by Montaigne's remark, and at once would have produced a handful of anecdotes to show him the error of his ways. Yet Montaigne accepts the old convention of the importance of a man's last hours. The day we die, he says, "is the master-day, the day that is the judge of all the other days": [53] a statement with which the Catholic Church would fully agree. But it is the master-day, not because it leads to heaven or hell, but because on that day one can prove one's nobility by being impervious to death. This was not a medieval, but a classical, view. In fact Montaigne, through all his inconsistencies, seems to be striving (as from one aspect the whole Renaissance was striving) to recapture the classical outlook — in this case an apparent disregard of death, the belief that to die is "but to endure one evil hour." At this period of his life, in other words, he was trying to scrape off the thick accretion of medieval teaching that had become fixed to the simpler doctrines. But he used, as he was forced to use, the medieval

---

so, it is no cowardice in me to believe it." See also ii, 21: "The highest degree, and the most natural, of bravely meeting death, is to look upon her not only without dismay, but unconcernedly, freely continuing one's wonted course of life even into her very lap."

53. Bk. i, 19.

method. He put the thought of death continually before him, just as the Middle Ages and the Reformation had done. Yet he did so, not that the moment of death might be increased in vividness, but that he might disregard it.

As time went on, his point of view grew still further away from medievalism, and he shook off the Stoicism which was, after all, fundamentally incompatible with his nature. In the early essays, such as the one I have been quoting, Montaigne speaks with scorn of the ordinary attitude to death. "The remedy of the vulgar is not to think of it, but from what brutish stupidity can proceed so gross a blindness?" Such disregard is nothing but "bestial nonchalance." Yet a few years later, it is just this "bestial nonchalance" that he advocates:

If you do not know how to die, do not let it trouble you; Nature will give you full and sufficient instructions when the time comes. She will do the business for you at the precise moment; do not burden your mind with the thought of it. . . . If we have known how to live bravely and tranquilly we shall know how to die bravely and tranquilly. They may brag as much as they please, that *the whole life of a Philosopher is a meditation on death* (Cicero). But it seems to me that it is, indeed, the end, but not the aim of life; it is its finality, its extremity, not however, its object.[54]

Nothing could be more contrary to late medieval teaching than this, and it shows how Montaigne, when considering matters that in a sense were a

54. Bk. III, 12.

medieval specialty, refused to accept the morbid convention which had weighed so heavily on previous generations. On the contrary, he achieved a position of complete independence, and it is because he expressed, in this matter as in others, the largely unconscious feeling of many of his contemporaries that his words have so great a meaning for our purpose.

But it would be a gross error to suppose that everybody always agreed with him. They may have wanted to, and when things were going well they probably did, but most people, when they began to think about serious matters, found the weight of the old teaching too heavy to be easily set aside. The moment doubt crept in, or ambition failed to be satisfied, or religious emotions were aroused, the world seemed a hollow place, and death the only fit subject for contemplation. We can find this admirably exemplified by Nashe's pamphlet, "Christs Teares over Jerusalem" (1593). Overcome by a fit of revulsion against the external splendor of his time, Nashe repeats again, though in more handsome language, those objurgations with which we are already so familiar. "Why doe wee raigne as Gods on the earth that are to be eaten with wormes?" he cries. "O what is beauty more than a wind-blowne bladder, that it should forget whereto it is borne? It is the foode of cloying-concupiscence, lyving, and the substance of the most noysome in-

fection, beeing dead." Death is everywhere, "yet
. . . why prepare wee not to die?" And he urges us,
in his elaborate and eloquent periods, to think of
how all our bravery shall perish, and to let the
"dampe and deadly terror" of the thought strike
deep into our souls.

The whole tone of the pamphlet is medieval, and
since it was written at just the moment when the
drama was beginning to reach its height, it is very
valuable for our study. It does not stand alone; it is
representative of a whole class of similar reversals.
Stubbes, Gosson, Rankins, Greene, Marston, Dekker, all in their various ways attacked the pride and
the worldly individualism their generation had developed. But Nashe's pamphlet — and he expresses
similar ideas in his other writings — shows more
clearly than any of these the significance that lies
behind them. The conscience of the new spirit was
not easy. It was overcome by moments of profound
repentance, and in those moments it reverted to
medievalism. The old moral was reiterated again;
think of death, for the world is an evil dream, and
only by dying can you enter into true life.

Here we may leave our preliminary discussion.
The thought of death was in the background of
everybody's mind at the end of the sixteenth century; it was at the core of orthodox religion, and unless he were a Montaigne, the moment a man began

to question the values expressed in the newer convention of fame and the contemporary love of worldly splendor, he fell back on the morality the old teaching implied, and tried, like Nashe, to think of death as the beginning of everything worthwhile. The love of worldly splendor itself put a new emphasis on death, for death, it seemed, brought to an end more wealth of life than before, and the greatness of its depredations made it more formidable than ever. As one looks back on the period it appears inevitable that when Elizabethan drama arose, the long stored emotional intensity about death, and the emotional friction caused by the divergent attitudes toward the subject, should become a chief dramatic resource, and that as a result man's attitude to one of the main facts of his existence should, in various subtle and revealing ways, be changed. How this is true it is now, among other things, our business to determine.

Chapter III

THE ELIZABETHAN DRAMA: LANGUAGE

"You cannot change a man's ideas without changing his vocabulary."

Wyndham Lewis

I

SO FAR we have been considering our subject solely from the historical point of view. But we must now approach it from a different direction. Elizabethan drama is not only a mine from which we may dig out expressions of past states of feeling; it is also a form of art, and it must be treated as a form of art before we try to draw any historical conclusions from what it says. All artistic achievement depends on three things: a medium, a content, and a technique; and since we are considering poetic drama, we must approach that drama through its medium of words, its content of emotive ideas, and its technical devices; we must for the time being put historical considerations aside. Only when we have done this, can we hope to understand the historical meaning of the Elizabethan dramatic treatment of death.

Gorboduc (1561), the first Elizabethan tragedy in English, does not give much indication of the future greatness of Elizabethan drama. As far as death is concerned the language of the play is merely a repe-

tition of the language of non-dramatic literature.
Death is personified as "pale" (act III); it is called
"dreadful" (act IV); worms are mentioned in connection with it (act III). The ideas are equally unoriginal: we hear of the necessity for revenge — that
ancient doctrine of an eye for an eye which was to
be so useful a convention for the Elizabethan drama
— we are told that life is "loathsome" (act IV); and
when a character is in trouble he expresses a desire
for death, which is then "sweet and welcome" to
him (act IV). We get a touch of one of the forms of
sentimentality when Marcella recounts the charms
of her dead hero (act IV); we have an expression of
the desire for fame (act v); we hear of the praise-
worthiness of the soldier's·death (act v).

All these are stock expressions and ideas; they
occur throughout sixteenth-century poetry. But
Gorboduc does not only repeat the platitudes of its
non-dramatic contemporaries, as we should of
course expect it to do; it also establishes a new set of
conventions of its own. These are as follows: first,
and perhaps most important, an "atmosphere" of
death is produced, which gives a tragic implication
to the action. This is done twice: by the mourners
of the dumb-show before act three, and by the
furies of the dumb-show before act four. Then, although no death, except in a dumb-show, takes
place on the stage, a definite attempt is made to
arouse emotion in the audience by describing a

death-bed scene. The death of Porrex (IV, 2), for example, is thus described:

> We . . .
>
> Wiped in vain with napkins next at hand
> The sudden streams of blood that flushed fast
> Out of the gaping wound. O what a look . . .
> He fix'd upon my face, which to my death
> Will never part from me, when with a braid
> A deep-fetch'd sigh he gave, and therewithal
> Clasping his hands, to heaven he cast his sight!
> And straight pale death pressing within his face,
> The flying ghost his mortal corpse forsook.

In addition to these specifically dramatic devices, there is an influence in this play which we have not previously met — the influence of Seneca. But though the play is obviously built along Senecan lines, the only thing that is distinctly Senecan about its treatment of death is that the deaths of the main characters occur behind the scenes, and are described by messengers. The verbal, moral, and emotional conventions, as we have seen, can all be paralleled in contemporary non-dramatic literature, and the chief technical innovation — the dumb-shows, and the impression of impending tragedy which they create — is not Senecan at all. We shall have more to say in another place about the Senecan influence on the treatment of death in Elizabethan drama; it will suffice, for the moment, to repeat for the drama as a whole what we have said about *Gorboduc* in particular: that as far as our subject is concerned, Seneca's effect was chiefly upon dramatic technique, hardly at all upon language, and only a little more upon ideas.

The way in which death is treated in *Gorboduc* is typical of all Elizabethan tragedy before Marlowe: the language is stiff and conventional, and if the authors felt any strong emotion, they were prevented from communicating it with much effectiveness by the crudity of their technique. Language was not yet the elastic and supple thing it was soon to become, and it would be a waste of time to linger over such plays as *Cambyses* or *The Misfortunes of Arthur*. We must therefore turn directly to the great period between 1588 and 1620 and examine the linguistic use of death which is to be found there in such ample and rewarding profusion.

2

In the popular literature of the fourteenth and fifteenth centuries the vocabulary used in connection with death is lean and impoverished; from all the literature of that time which I have examined — religious lyrics, saints' lives, and some seventy metrical romances — I was able to harvest only five adjectives which were applied to death: doleful, horrible, cold, cruel, and dreadful.[1] But the poetry

1. There are a few conventional phrases, besides these adjectives, applied to death in medieval literature, but they are not many. Death shoots a dart, he uses a mace and a sword, he is called a thief. The phrase "dead as a door-nail" also appears fairly frequently. But there is nothing fresh or original about such

of the sixteenth century yields different results. Death is there called cruel, dark, devouring, loathsome, miserable, horrible, cursed, undaunted, spiteful, greedy, outrageous, hateful, dreadful, grim, pale, untamed, lingering, slothful, darting, careless, grisly, ghastly, dogged, fell, cankered, lean, stern, ugly, insulting, fearful, prodigious, strange, impartial, meager, sinful, and foul. A formidable list, and, be it noted, inclusive only of adjectives; metaphors, similes, epithets of all kinds exist in equal profusion.

Anyone acquainted, even superficially, with Elizabethan literature, would naturally expect this wealth of vocabulary. The English language took on a more elaborate texture in the sixteenth century than it had ever possessed before: words were borrowed from foreign languages, from slang, from all the occupations of man.[2] No Elizabethan writer was content with saying a thing simply; he dressed

---

expressions. The only author who has anything new to produce in the way of similes is the anonymous translator of the *Laud Troy Book*, and the newness of his similes can hardly be called imaginative. The following account of the fight of Neoptolemus and Archilogus is typical:

"Ayther gaff other suche a kayl
That they fflowen over the hors tayl
Opon that playn, as it were two rattes,
They lay ston-stille as two cattes."

(vv. 6783 ff.)

2. The Elizabethan translations throw much light on this fact. See F. O. Matthiessen, *Translation: an Elizabethan Art*, Cambridge, Massachusetts, 1931, *passim*.

his style as he dressed his body, with as much richness as possible. It gave him pleasure to heap adjective upon adjective, to toss his bright words extravagantly in the air, to shower his thoughts with metaphor. Above all, the Elizabethans were gifted with a remarkable facility for vizualization, and an abstraction rarely occurred to their minds without being seen as a vivid concrete thing.

Of no abstraction was this more true than of death. The late medieval emphasis on the skeleton had created a personified image, which almost automatically attracted to itself the wealth of adjective and metaphor the sixteenth century was so exuberantly discovering. We rarely find the word "death" used alone; it is qualified by some descriptive phrase which at once brings it sharply before our eyes. As we read the great Elizabethans we feel, through their use of language alone, that death haunted their imaginations, and released a wealth of expression that has not yet been equaled.

3

It will be convenient to open our investigation by taking one or two passages and tracing their parallels. We may begin with one of the most familiar, the lines from the last speech of Romeo:

> Shall I believe
> That unsubstantial Death is amorous,
> And that the lean abhorred monster keeps
> Thee here in dark to be his paramour?

Now if the reader has examined the list of adjectives given above, he will have found that they fall roughly into two classes: those which are applicable to death as an abstraction, and those which are applicable to a clearly defined image. To the first class belong such words as "cold" and "pale," to the second, such words as "grisly," "meager," and "lean." Death is conceived as it affects the body, leaving the corpse pale and foul, and it is seen as a lean-ribbed skeleton, a personality as grisly as the effects of its outrageous depredations. But the two notions are intimately bound together, and it is often difficult to tell which is being thought of; the abstraction and its personification are almost one.

This is very clearly brought out by Romeo's speech. He first thinks of death in general terms — he is without a body, "unsubstantial"; but immediately, with the use of the word "amorous," the transition, so typically Shakespearean, is made to the concrete, and the conceit is made vivid to our minds by being personified. What this personification was is obvious: it is the skeleton which the late Middle Ages had adopted as their symbol, and which grinned and danced on the walls of so many sixteenth-century buildings.[3]

3. We may here remember, as F. Douce pointed out in his *Holbein's Dance of Death*, London, 1858, p. 46, that there was a Dance of Death painted in the church at Stratford. Douce calls attention to the lines in *Measure for Measure*, III, I, 11–12: "Merely thou art death's fool," etc., and remarks on the frequency with which death, in the pictures, was invested with the fool's livery.

The chief words used to call up this connotation, "lean monster," are each part of tradition also. Marlowe, for instance, makes Tamburlaine speak as follows (*2 Tamb.*, v, 3):

> See, where my slave, the ugly *monster* death,
> Shaking and quivering, pale and wan for fear,
> Stands aiming at me with his murdering dart;

a passage that seems to be almost a direct description of a picture from a Dance of Death. Shirley uses the same word (*Traitor*, IV, 2):

> I never
> Thought death the *monster* that weak men have fancied.

And it is frequent in other writers.[4]

The adjective "lean" is also common. Dekker, who considered tobacco an abomination, calls death "that *lean* tawny face tobacconist" (*Old Fortunatus*, I, 1); and again, far more magnificently:

> And though mine arm should conquer twenty worlds,
> There's a *lean* fellow beats all conquerors,
>   (*Old Fort.*, I, 1)

a passage which has a considerable interest in itself, for it shows what a slight hint was needed in order

4. See *2 Tamb.*, v, 3:
> "The monarch of the earth,
> And *eyeless monster* that torments my soul."
Shakespeare plays with this image of death as an ugly monster very effectively in *Cymbeline*, v, 3:
> "I, in mine own woe charm'd
> Could not find death where I did hear him groan,
> Nor feel him where he struck: being an *ugly monster*,
> 'Tis strange he hides him in fresh cups, soft beds,
> Sweet words. . . ."

to make it clear that death was meant. The audience, accustomed to hearing death referred to as "lean," would at once know who the "lean fellow" was, and on this knowledge Dekker could rely. The commonness of the convention enabled him to be suggestive; and it is its suggestiveness that makes this line such fine poetry — a fact which, as we shall see later, throws light on the connection between poetry and convention.

Marston also speaks of death as "lean" (*Insatiate Countess*, III, 1):

> *Lean* death, swoll'n big with the Hellespont,
> In bleak Leander's body;

and again, in the same act:

> I see *lean* death, with eyes imaginary,
> Stand fearfully before me.

And to pass outside the drama for a moment, we find Samuel Rowlands speaking of death as a "*lean* knave."[5] It was a very common expression.

The second adjective used by Romeo, "abhorred," has an even larger number of parallels than "lean." The word itself may not be so frequently employed, but its synonyms occur plentifully enough. The non-dramatic literature speaks of death as loathsome, horrible, hateful, dreadful, grisly, ghastly, etc. — all adjectives which have a

5. *Battel betweene Time and Death*, ed. Hunterian Club (1874), p. 34: Time speaks to Death: "Th'art a *leane* knave."

feeling of abhorrence back of them. Marlowe calls
death "grisly":

> Where'er I come the fatal sisters sweat,
> And *grisly* death, by running to and fro
> To do their ceaseless homage to my sword,
>
> (*1 Tamb.*, V, 2)

and he calls him "ghastly":

> and now doth *ghastly* death
> With greedy talons gripe my bleeding heart.
>
> (*Ibid.*, I, 7)

Beaumont and Fletcher make one of their characters say to another: "Death is not so *terrible* as
thou" (*Maid's Tragedy*, V, 4); and the ugliness of
death (apart from the quotations we have already
given) is mentioned with considerable frequency.[6]

It is thus evident that Shakespeare's words, "lean
abhorred monster," are not by any means original
with him, but are part of the common stock of expressions and associations, handed down by tradition, from which the writer could select as he
pleased. The same thing is true of the idea which
lies behind Shakespeare's words: the notion that

---

6. *1 Tamb.*, III, 2:
> "Upon his brows was pourtrayed *ugly* death."

2 Tamb., III, 4:
> "Now, *ugly* Death, stretch out thy sable wings."

Marston, *Malcontent*, II, 3:
> "Death and shame, two of the *ugliest* shapes
> That can confound a soul."

See Shakespeare, *King John*, V, 4:
> "Have I not *hideous* death within my view."

when a person dies, he or she has some kind of physical union with death. Frequently the character goes to meet death as if to a wedding. This is an old conception, and may be found in the Greek Anthology. "No husband but Death did Clearista receive on her bridal night," [7] say Meleager. Shakespeare seems particularly fond of this notion. Lear uses it: "I will die bravely as a *bridegroom*" (*Lear*, IV, 6); Antony uses it: "I will be a *bridegroom* in my death" (*Antony and Cleopatra*, IV, 12); and Claudio cries, reversing the application of the simile: "If I must die, I will encounter darkness as a *bride*" (*Measure for Measure*, III, 1). So Maria, in Marston's *Malcontent* (V, 5), on learning she must die, says:

> soul, now thy wish thou hast;
> Die like a *bride*.

Shirley employs this convention more elaborately than anyone else; but writing as he did at the end of the great period, he no longer possessed that gift of concentration and intensity which his predecessors had known how to use so admirably, and he takes the conception of death as a bridegroom and expands it out of all proper proportion. The result is momentarily effective, but when we think it over, we realize that rhetoric has taken the place of poetry, and theatricality the place of drama. Amidea (*Traitor*, IV, 2) is speaking:

7. VII, 182. Quoted F. P. Weber, *Aspects of Death*, London, 1918, pp. 324–325.

            I shall be married shortly.
Pisano: To whom?
Amidea: To one whom you have all heard talk of,
            Your fathers knew him well: one, who will never
            Give cause I should suspect him to forsake me;
            A constant lover, one whose lips, though cold,
            Distil chaste kisses: though our bridal bed
            Be not adorned with roses, 'twill be green;
            We shall have virgin laurel, cypress, yew,
            To make us garlands; though no pine do burn,
            Our nuptial shall have torches, and our chamber
            Shall be cut out of marble, where we'll sleep,
            Free from all care forever: Death, my lord,
            I hope, shall be my husband.

Thus we can see, when Shakespeare makes Romeo wonder whether death keeps Juliet as his paramour, that his words are a variation on a common notion, and that without it, the bitterness which the passage has would lose its force. Such a use of convention is one of the most striking things about the period we are considering.

So much, then, for Romeo's speech. Let us now take another short passage and subject it to the same treatment. The following lines from Dekker's play, _The Honest Whore_ (pt. 1, 1, 1), will serve our purpose. The Duke is speaking to the disconsolate lover, Hippolito, who believes his lady to be dead:

Duke: Nay, nay, be but patient;
           For why death's hand hath sued a strict divorce
           'Twixt her and thee: what's beauty but a corse?
           What but fair sand-dust are earth's purest forms?
           Queen's bodies are but trunks to put in worms.
Matheo: Speak no more sentences, my good lord.

Matheo recognizes that the Duke's remarks are platitudes, and it is this recognition which makes them so interesting to us. For it means that we have here, in a more or less unsmelted state, the raw material which in the passage from Shakespeare had already been turned into poetic steel.

"Death's hand" was a common expression. Turberville had used it in his *Epitaphes* (1567): "Nothing prevailes against his [death's] hatefull *hands*," [8] and Daniel brought it into his "Funerall Poeme upon the Death of the . . . Earle of Devonshire":

> Now that the *hand* of death hath layd thee there
> Where neither greatness, pompe, nor grace, we see,
> Nor any differences of earth. [9]

But it was far more frequent in the drama:

> It is a pain, beyond the *hand of death*,
> To be in doubt,

says Amintor in Beaumont and Fletcher's *Maid's Tragedy* (II, 1); and there are at least six more instances of the phrase, four of them in Shakespeare.[10]

---

8. Ed. J. P. Collier (n. d.), p. 245, "Epitaph on . . . Maister Tufton."

9. *Works*, ed. Grosart, Spenser Soc. (1885), I, 171.

10. E.g., Massinger and Dekker, *Virgin Martyr*, IV, 3:
> "Ere the iron *hand* of death close up my eyes."

Ibid.:
> "Death, looking on her constancy, would forget
> The use of his inevitable *hand*."

Richard II, III, 1:
> "See them deliver'd over
> To execution and the *hand* of death."

It is a natural metaphor, and had other forms. Being seized by death's hand was like being seized by the hand of the constable when one was arrested. The phrase "death's arrest" is found fairly frequently in medieval literature; and it occurs in sixteenth-century lyrics also.[11] When it is employed in the drama, the same thing happens to it that happened to so many other platitudinous phrases. After having been used for centuries in a flat, second-hand way, it suddenly assumes a new and vigorous expression. Shakespeare had already transformed and amplified it in one of his sonnets (LXXIV):

> But be contented: when that *fell arrest*
> Without all bail shall carry me away,

and in *Hamlet* (v, 2) he used it again, carrying the metaphor further still:

> Had I but time, — as this *fell sergeant, death,*
> Is strict in his *arrest,* — O! I could tell you . . . .

---

1 Henry IV, IV, 1:
> "Talk not of dying: I am out of fear
> Of death or death's *hand* for this one half year."

Ibid., V, 4:
> "O! I could prophesy,
> But that the earthy and cold *hand* of death
> Lies on my tongue."

Antony and Cleopatra, IV, 9:
> "The *hand* of death hath raught him."

11. E.g., Whetstone, *Rock of Regard* (1576), ed. J. P. Collier (n. d.), p. 318:
> "He was soudainly *arested* with death."

Rowlands, *Battel betweene Time and Death*, ed. cit., p. 34: Time says to Death:
> "Th'art a leane knave: Take witnes and *arest* me."

The image, as usual, is kept alive by being personified. Chapman does the same thing (*All Fools*, 1, 2) with remarkable vividness:

> And finding him her debtor, do but send
> Her *sergeant, John Death*, to *arrest* his body.

The next remark of Dekker's Duke, that death has "sued a strict divorce 'Twixt her and thee," is a variant of the simile about marriage that we discussed above. The expression is by no means unusual. Perhaps it is a new application of the aged notion that the soul and body are divorced at death, in which fashion Whetstone had used it: "And now, good death, with speede *divorce* my soule from lothed life";[12] but it is more likely that it is merely a rewording of the familiar fact that death separates one person from another.

The Duke's next platitude, "What's beauty but a corse," may, as we know, be found over and over again. It was the keynote of all medieval teaching:

> A blast of winde, a momentarie breath,
> A watrie bubble simbolizde with ayre,
> A sunne-blowne rose, but for a season fayre,
> A ghostly glaunce, a skeleton of death. . . .
> Is Man.[13]

H. Gifford, "Posie of Gillowflowers," in *Miscellanies of the Fuller Worthies' Library*, London, 1871, i, 342:
> "But Death *arestes* us by the way."

Ibid., p. 405:
> ". . . when death shall *arest* me."

12. *Rock of Regard, ed. cit.*, p. 99.

13. Barnaby Barnes, "Divine Centurie of Spiritual Sonnets" (1595), in T. Park, *Heliconia*, London, 1815, ii, son. LXXX.

It is quite unnecessary to produce further parallels. The same holds true of the Duke's subsidiary remark: "What but fair sand-dust are earth's purest forms?" The well-known passage in Job at once recurs to mind, and its echo in the Anglican burial service — "dust to dust." "What have you done," asks Rosencrantz of Hamlet (*Hamlet*, IV, 2), "with the dead body?" "*Compounded* it with *dust*, whereto 'tis kin." Henry IV as he is dying asks: "Only *compound* me with forgotten *dust*" (*2 Henry IV*, IV, 5).

Dust and worms are closely connected, and it is interesting to note with what effect the common theme could be varied (*Hamlet*, IV, 3):

King: Now, Hamlet, where's Polonius?
Hamlet: At supper.
King: At supper! Where?
Hamlet: Not where he eats, but where he is eaten: a certain convocation of politic worms are e'en at him.

And Dekker, perhaps remembering Shakespeare, writes as follows (*1 Honest Whore*, I, 1):

On Thursday buried! and on Monday died!
Quick haste, byrlady; sure her winding sheet
Was laid out 'fore her body; and the worms
That now must feast with her, were even bespoke,
And solemnly invited like strange guests.

In both these examples the ironic tampering with a common convention gives the writing a tang which makes it an emotional success.

Thus all the remarks made by Dekker's Duke are platitudinous; they were the sort of thing anybody could have produced at a moment's notice, and Dekker recognized the fact not only by definitely calling them "sentences," but also by putting them in rhyme — a convenient way the Elizabethans had of marking anything as conventionally uplifting.

With these illustrative passages behind us, let us now turn to an examination of the many other words and phrases which the Elizabethans applied to death. The characteristics of a warrior, which were so strikingly his in the Middle Ages, are less obvious in the Elizabethan drama. He has, indeed, his usual weapons:

> Do not, therefore,
> Ascribe the perturbation of my soul
> To a servile fear of death: I oft have view'd
> All kinds of his inevitable *darts*.[14]

And he has a mace [15] as well. But on the whole the warrior-like appurtenances of death are conspicuous in the drama largely by their absence; other details were substituted.

The scythe of death, for instance, occurs. Shakespeare refers to it (*Antony and Cleopatra*, III, 11):

> The next time I do fight
> I'll make death love me, for I will contend
> Even with his pestilent *scythe*.

---

14. Massinger, *Unnatural Combat*, II, 1.

15. Nashe and Marlowe, *Tragedy of Dido*, II, 1: "Pale Death's stony *mace*." Connected with this is the notion of death's stroke: Peele, *Edward I*, 5: "Whom naught can daunt, no, not the *stroke*

Shirley has a variation:

> Death's a devouring gamester
> And sweeps up all. . . .
> No Amidea . . . the *sickle* shall not touch
> A flower that grows so fair upon his stalk —
>
> (*Traitor*, v, 1)

a quotation which, like so many, illustrates another point beside that it is used for. There are many personifications of death; not only is he a gamester, as here, or a "tobacconist" (see above, p. 73); he is also compared to a harpy (*1 Tamb.*, II, 7):

> and now doth ghastly death
> With greedy talons gripe my bleeding heart,
> And like a harpy tires on my life.

Following no doubt the account in the Apocalypse, he is a rider: "Death rides in triumph, Drusus," says one of the characters in Fletcher's *Bonduca* (III, 5); and either Massinger or Dekker, in their play of the *Virgin Martyr* (IV, 2), uses exactly the same phrase: "Death this day rides in triumph, Theophilus." Marlowe calls death "the monarch of the earth" (*2 Tamb.*, v, 3), and speaks of "the wrath and tyranny of death" (*ibid.*). Mendoza, in Marston's *Insatiate Countess* (III, 1), with similar phrasing, remarks:

> Though death be entered in this tower of flesh,
> He is not conqueror; my heart stands out,
> And yields to thee, scorning his *tyranny*!

---

of death"; *Antony and Cleopatra*, v, 2: "The *stroke* of death is as a lover's pinch."

Talbot, in *1 Henry VI*, iv, 7, repeats this notion in connection with another:

> Thou *antick*, death, which laugh'st us here to scorn,
> Anon, from thy insulting *tyranny* . . .
> Two Talbots . . .
> In thy despite shall 'scape mortality —

a passage which at once recalls the famous speech of Richard II (iii, 2):

> within the hollow crown
> That rounds the mortal temples of a king
> Keeps Death his court, and there the *antick* sits,
> Scoffing his state and grinning at his pomp. . . .

There cannot be a moment's doubt as to where the picture of death as an "antick," who laughs everybody to scorn, comes from. In just this character he appears in the Dances of Death; and Holbein's woodcut of death and the Queen, shows him clad in full "antick" regalia, with cap and bells.[16] It is worth while reminding ourselves again that (on Stowe's authority) there was a painting of the Dance of Death at Stratford-on-Avon.

The personifications of death in the drama are almost as numerous as the various human occupations. We have a reference to death's thief-like characteristics (which are so plentifully mentioned in medieval literature [17]) in *2 Tamb.*, v, 3:

16. See *The Dance of Death*, ed. Austin Dobson, London, 1892.
17. Chaucer so describes him in *The Pardoner's Tale*:
"There cam a privee *theef* men clepe deeth."

> See, where my slave, the ugly monster, death
> Stands aiming at me with his murdering dart
> And, when I look away, comes *stealing* on;

Dekker refers to death as a painter: "Death's the best *painter*, then" (*1 Honest Whore*, IV, 1); and also: "I see Death's a good *trencherman*, he can eat coarse homely meat, as well as the daintiest" (*2 Honest Whore*, I, 2); and Shakespeare, in a magnificent passage, speaks as follows:

> it is great
> To do that thing which ends all other deeds,
> Which shackles accidents, and bolts up change,
> Which sleeps, and never palates more the dug,
> The beggar's *nurse*, and Caesar's.
>
> *(Antony and Cleopatra*, v, 2)

So in *Cymbeline* (v, iv) we hear of "the sure *physician* death." But, though he is so frequently personified in metaphor, death in person comes, to my knowledge, only once on the stage; he, with Love and Fortune, form the chorus to Kyd's *Soliman and Perseda*. How he was costumed, there is unfortunately nothing to tell us; all we know is that he has a "sable dart." He ends the play with a list of those whom he has killed, in true medieval style.

That he was represented as a skeleton, however, we can assume from analogy. Marlowe speaks of the "*eyeless* monster that torments my soul" (*2 Tamb.*, v, 3),[18] with that image undoubtedly before him,

18. See *Cymbeline*, v, 4:
   "Your death has eyes in's head, then;
   I have not seen him so pictured."

and when Shakespeare wrote of "bare-ribb'd death" (*King John*, v, 2) he unquestionably had the figure of the skeleton in his mind.

In the great majority of cases, then, death was personified as something fearful. Even non-committal adjectives, such as "cold" or "pale," when used in connection with death, were plainly there to produce an emotional shudder. The word "death" itself, with no descriptive adjectives attached, called up fear. "I cannot abide this word 'death,'" says Depazzi in Shirley's *Traitor* (iii, 1), and Webster's Brachiano cries (*White Devil*, v, 3):

> On pain of death, let no man name death to me:
> It is a word infinitely terrible.

4

As I have observed, it is frequently difficult to separate those occasions on which death is thought of concretely from those on which it is referred to as an abstraction. But nevertheless there are certain expressions and allusions where no concrete image appears, and where, perhaps as a result, the emotion of fear does not seem to be so generally predominant. The chief fear-provoking phrase of this kind is a common one: "death's black shade." It is connected with two conceptions, the fear of the dark, and the descriptions of the other world. The first, of course, is so universal that it needs no emphasis. As for the second, we find Homer speaking (in Chapman's translation) of "Pluto's dark house," of the "black region";[19] Vergil of the "*tenebrosa palus Acheronte*," "bis Stygios innare lacus, bis *nigra* videre Tartara," and

> Ibant *obscuri* sola sub *nocte* per *umbram*,[20]
> Perque domos Ditis vacuas et inania regna.

Seneca too has many remarks about the darkness of Hades — "*opaca* . . . loca":

> Est in recessu Tartari *obscuro* locus,
> Quem *gravibus umbris* spissa caligo alligat.[21]

And it was perhaps because of Seneca that the Elizabethans were so fond of using the phrase. "How art thou changed in death's *black shade*," says Hieronimo, imagining his son to be standing before him (*Spanish Tragedy*, III, 13). In fact the connection of the phrase with classical convention caused it to be used frequently, in imitation of classical authors, as a metaphor for the other world. Francesco in Webster's *White Devil* (v, 2) says of Brachiano, whom he has just poisoned, "This shall his passage to the *black lake* further" — words which seem almost a translation of the line in Vergil quoted above. A considerable effect of awe could be produced by reference to darkness, as when the ghost of Bussy D'Ambois appears (Chapman, *Revenge of Bussy*, v, 1):

19. *Odyssey*, bks. x and xi.
20. *Aeneid*, bk. vi.
21. *Hercules Furens*, vv. 708 ff.

Up from the chaos of *eternal night*
(To which the whole digestion of the world
Is now returning) once more I ascend.[22]

These lines bring us to another association, one intimately connected with the foregoing: that be-

22. In this same connection, see also Middleton, *Fair Quarrel*, II, I:

"In that *dark* depth where all bad quarrels sink
Never to rise again."

Fletcher, *Thierry and Theodoret*, IV, I:

"For in the silent grave . . .
Dust and an endless *darkness*."

Middleton (*Changeling*, V, 3) uses the blackness in a far more medieval fashion:

"Rehearse again
Your scene of lust, that you may be perfect
When you shall come to act it to the *black* audience,
Where howls and gnashings shall be music to you."

For the blackness of medieval devils, see my article, "Chaucer's Hell," *Speculum*, II (1927), 194.

3 Henry VI, II, 6:

"*Dark cloudy death* o'ershades his beams of life."

3 Henry VI, V, 2:

"These eyes, that now are dimm'd with *death's black veil*."

Richard III, I, 3:

"My son, now in the *shade* of death;
Whose bright out-shining beams thy cloudy wrath
Hath in eternal *darkness* folded up."

Richard III, I, 4:

"I pass'd . . .
Unto the kingdom of perpetual *night*."

Richard III, V, 3:

"Lest his son George fall
Into the *blind* cave of eternal *night*."

There is, of course, considerable difference in the way these various descriptions of darkness are applied. But they are all held together by the fact that death is connected with them, whether it be that all is dark in the grave, or that darkness is a well-known feature of hell, in medieval, as well as classical legend.

tween death and night. This was extremely common. Hieronimo (*Spanish Tragedy*, IV, 4), as he recounts his son's murder by Lorenzo and Balthasar, says:

> There merciless they butcher'd up my boy,
> In *black, dark night*, to pale, dim, cruel death —

a quotation which could not be bettered as an illustration of how meaningless the common adjectives applied to death became in the hands of a second-class poet. "Black night o'ershade thy day, and death thy life!" exclaims Lady Anne when Richard makes love to her (*Richard III*, I, 2); and Bolingbroke curses the murderer in *Richard II* (V, 6): "With Cain go wander through the shade of night." This remark is associated with at least three interwoven traditions: that murder is punished, that there is something horrible in the dark, and, connected with the form of punishment, that there is darkness in hell. So Juliet, before swallowing the potion which will make her appear dead, wonders, should she survive its effects, whether "the horrible conceit of *death and night*" will not make her mad (*Romeo and Juliet*, IV, 2). Macbeth (III, 2) invokes "seeling night" that his murder of Banquo may be performed in an appropriate atmosphere. Night is, of course, the fit time for deeds of murder, and it was used in many Elizabethan tragedies for this purpose.

Even more common than the connection between death and night is that between death and sleep. Homer speaks of the "twin brethren, Sleep and Death" (*Iliad*, xvi, 671). Hesiod has: "Night indeed brought forth hateful Fate and black Doom and Death, and brought forth Sleep and gave birth to the race of Dreams" (*Theog.*, 211), and again: "the other one, destructive Night, veiled in musky mist, [holding] in her hands Sleep, the brother of Death" (*Theog.*, 756). The relationship between night, death, and sleep is thus a very ancient one; sleep and death are connected hundreds of times in classic authors. Such parallels, however, were somewhat too restful for the violence of medieval opinions about death, and the analogy between death and sleep is rarely found in the Middle Ages. But it was extremely common in the sixteenth century: "O Death, O Death, rock me asleep," cries an anonymous lyricist in 1536.[23] Daniel's famous sonnet beginning:

> Care-charmer Sleep, son of the sable Night,
> Brother to Death, in silent darkness born,[24]

seems almost a translation of Hesiod. Yet death was not always referred to as sleep's brother. Grimald speaks of "Sleeps doolful *sister*, who is wont for no

23. Norman Ault, *Elizabethan Lyrics*, London, 1925, p. 9.
24. See the song in Fletcher's *Valentinian*:
    "Care-charming Sleep, thou easer of all woes,
    Brother to Death — "

respect to spare," [25] and Sackville, in his Induction to the *Mirror for Magistrates*, makes the relationship more vague: "By him lay heavy Sleepe, the *cosin* of Death." [26]

This connection of sleep and death was, in the drama, the most platitudinous of all the platitudes we have been discussing. It is almost as rare to find an Elizabethan tragedy without a reference to it as to find a comedy without a joke about cuckolds. Isabella's maid, for instance, in the *Spanish Tragedy* (III, 8) comforts her mistress as follows:

> Good madam, affright not thus yourself
> With outrage for your son Horatio:
> He *sleeps* in quiet in the Elysian fields.

Marlowe (*1 Tamb.*, III, 2) has:

> And let Agydas by Agydas die
> And with this stab *slumber* eternally;

Shakespeare (*Macbeth*, III, 2):

> Duncan is in his grave;
> After life's fitful fever he *sleeps* well.

Fletcher's Thierry (*Thierry and Theodoret*, IV, 1), questioning the veiled lady he is about to sacrifice, speaks in a manner which should now be entirely familiar to us; he is describing death:

25. "Epitaph of . . . Margaret Lee, 1555," *Tottel's Miscellany*, ed. H. E. Rollins, Cambridge, Massachusetts, 1928, p. 109.

26. *Mirror*, ed. J. Haslewood, London, 1815, II, 320, st. 41. For a detailed comparison of sleep and death see *Gascoigne's Goodnyghte*, quoted above, p. 56.

> Nor nothing is, but all oblivion,
> Dust and an endless darkness; and dare you, woman,
> Desire this place?

Ordella: 'Tis of all *sleeps* the sweetest.

It is quite unnecessary to give further instances; the reader can find them for himself in almost any play. But before we pass on, it will be interesting to remind ourselves of the most famous use of this old convention, where, instead of being thoughtlessly repeated, it is seized upon with fresh vividness, and all its implications are thoroughly described:

> To die: to sleep;
> No more; and, by a sleep to say we end
> The heart-ache and the thousand natural shocks
> That flesh is heir to, 'tis a consummation
> Devoutly to be wish'd. To die, to sleep;
> To sleep: perchance to dream: ay, there's the rub;
> For in that sleep of death what dreams may come
> When we have shuffled off this mortal coil,
> Must give us pause.

Another popular manner of referring to death, as I have illustrated in discussing *Gorboduc*, was to describe it as "sweet" or "welcome." This was a description used very frequently by melancholy and lyrical lovers. The Earl of Surrey (like Chaucer in the *Book of the Duchess*) met a lover lamenting under a palm tree:

> Wherwith he turned him round, and gasping oft for breath,
> Into his armes a tree he raught, and sayd, *welcome my death* . . .
> Thus, in this wofull state, he yelded up the ghost.[27]

---

27. *Tottel's Miscellany, ed. cit.*, p. 17.

So Juliet, in Painter's version of her story, finding
Romeo dead, pricked herself with Romeo's dagger,
". . . sayinge with feeble and pitiful voice: 'Ah
death the end of sorrow, and beginning of felicity,
thou art most hartely *welcome*.'" [28] In the drama
words like these are also used when a character is in
difficulty — though that difficulty is not necessarily
caused by love. Marlowe's Olympia (*2 Tamb.*,
III, 4), for instance, when her husband has been
killed, speaks as follows:

> Death, whither art thou gone, that both we live?
> Come back agin, *sweet* death, and strike us both;

Charlemont, in Tourneur's *Atheist's Tragedy* (IV, 3),
having prevented D'Amville from raping Castabella, remarks:

> Now, *sweet* Death,
>   I'll bid thee *welcome*.

In *Nero* (III, 6) we have a slight variant:

> The gods sure keep it hid from us that live,
> How *sweet* death is, because we should go on,
> And be their bails.

28. *Palace of Pleasure*, ed. J. Jacobs, London, 1890, tom. II,
nov. 25. See Nicholas Breton, "A Smale Handfull of Fragrant
Flowers" (1575), in T. Park, *Heliconia*, London, 1815, I, 120:
    "And doost thou then, sweete Death! approche so neare?
        Welcome, my friend, and ease of all my woe;"
Gorgeous Gallery, ed. H. E. Rollins, Cambridge, Massachusetts,
1926, p. 37: "The Lover, having sustayned overmuch wrong at
his Ladyes hands wisheth speedy death;" *Mirror for Magistrates*,
ed. cit., I, 41, "Albanact," st. 70:
    "And farewell all my subjectes, farewell breath,
        Farewell ten thowsand times, and *welcome* death."

There were several other ways of referring to death, which are slightly (though only slightly) more original than these. Not infrequently death is a journey or a voyage to another land:

> The undiscover'd country from whose bourne
> No traveller returns.

Webster uses this ancient metaphor **twice**. Vittoria, as she dies, says (*White Devil*, v, 6):

> My soul, like to a ship in a black storm,
> Is driven, I know not whither.

And Bosola (*Duchess of Malfi*, v, 4):

> Let worthy minds ne'er stagger in distrust
> To suffer death or shame for what is just:
> Mine is another *voyage*.

Alsemero in Middleton's *Changeling* (v, 3) tells De Flores:

> Clip your adulteress freely, 'tis the pilot
> Will guide you to the *mare mortuum*
> Where you shall sink to fathoms bottomless;

and Kent, at the end of *Lear*, uses the same convention:

> I have a *journey*, sir, shortly to go;
> My master calls me, I must not say no.

Death is also spoken of as resembling a mist — a comparison which reminds us of Homer's description of it as a "black cloud" (*Iliad*, xx, 417–418). For example, Tamburlaine (*2 Tamb.*, ii, 4) refers to Zenocrate's being "all dazzled with the hellish *mists* of death"; Shirley's Cardinal dies with similar words on his lips (*Cardinal*, v, 3):

> My wings that flag may catch the wind; but 'tis
> In vain, the *mist* is risen, and there's none
> To steer my wandering bark.

The number of ways there are to die are also frequently mentioned in the drama. "How many several ways hath death to surprise us!" Montaigne had exclaimed (I, 20); and Webster's Duchess of Malfi, thinking of Sir Philip Sidney's phrase (*Arcadia*, III, 3), "the house of Death had so many doores, as she would easilie flie into it," echoes him:

> I know death hath ten thousand several doors
> For men to take their exits.
>
> (*Duchess of Malfi*, IV, 2)

"Death hath a thousand doors to let out life," cries Massinger's Almira (*A Very Woman*, v, 4); and Diocletian, in *The Virgin Martyr* (v, 2), remarks:

> Death shall put on a thousand shapes at once
> And so appear before thee.

According to Mr. Cunliffe,[29] the phrasing of this notion had its origin in Seneca, who has the following passage in his *Thebais* (151–153):

> ubique mors est. Optume hoc cavit deus,
> eripere vitam nemo non homini potest,
> at nemo mortem: *mille* ad hanc *aditus* patent.

---

29. *The Influence of Seneca on Elizabethan Tragedy*, London, 1893, pp. 23 ff. See also M. C. Bradbrook, *Themes and Conventions of*

Cunliffe cites passages from *The Misfortunes of Arthur*, *Antonio's Revenge*, *Love's Cruelty*, and other plays which say the same thing. These, together with those I have just quoted, show how common the phrase was, and like most of the common phrases, it was once or twice revitalized into fine poetry by being looked at in a new way. This time it was Marston who felt its truth, and gave it life by seeing it in relation to a fresh set of associations (*Antonio and Mellida*, III, 2):

> Each man takes hence life, but no man death:
> He's a good fellow, and keeps open house:
> A *thousand thousand* ways lead to his *gate*,
> To his wide-mouthed porch, when niggard life
> Hath but one little, little wicket through.

The passage illustrates another image as well. Death as a gate — *mors janua vitae* — was a trite expression in the Middle Ages, and Peele had used it in his *Edward I* (sc. 1):

> O God, my God, the brightness of my day,
> How oft hast thou preserved thy servant safe,
> By sea and land, yea, in the *gates of death*!

In fact we may see here how, in Marston's mind, one conventional expression followed another: he thought of the many ways of dying in connection with the familiar notion of death as a gate, which had itself been called to mind by his reference to

---

Elizabethan Tragedy, Cambridge, England, 1935, pp. 89–90, for further discussion of this platitude.

death's "house"; a picture of some great mansion he had once seen must have flashed before his mind, and he saw its wide entrance as it would be when many guests were expected, and its small wicket buried in the door when the gates were shut; he applied the image to what he was writing about, and the combination of convention, visual memory, and the emotion which the subject of death aroused, produced poetry.

There is one more point to be noticed about this passage: Marston's use of the word "fellow." This word derives its flavor from the fact that it was originally applied to a base person, and has never quite lost its low connections, while at the same time it refers to something important. The result is a kind of wry irony which is very effective when the word is used about death. "There's a lean *fellow* beats all conquerors," says Dekker, and again (*1 Honest Whore*, IV, I; Hippolito is addressing a skull):

> But here's a *fellow*; that which he lays on
> Till doomsday alters not complexion.

The emotional twinge given by the word is as easily recognizable as it is difficult to define.

5

Such, briefly described, is the richness of the Elizabethan vocabulary about death. Its wealth stands out particularly clearly when compared

to the word-impoverishment of the Middle Ages.
Though the Elizabethans used, with practically no
exceptions, the expressions the Middle Ages had
used, they added to them enormously; they piled up
adjectives and similes, metaphors and allusions, in
a way the Middle Ages had not dreamed of. The
word itself was used in that full-blown and baroque
way which is so typically Elizabethan:

> No such discourse is pleasant in mine ears,
> But that where every period ends with death,
> And every line begins with death again.[30]

And many writers beside Marlowe used death for
the sake of hyperbole. When Catiline wants to give
a sense of importance to his actions, he exclaims:

> Methinks I see Death and the Furies waiting
> What we will do.[31]

Francisco, in Massinger's *Duke of Milan* (II, 1), enforces his protestations of affection as strongly as he
can:

> Be it death,
> And death with torments tyrants ne'er found out,
> Yet I must say, I love you.

Such expressions are very common. Ford's Giovanni ('*Tis Pity She's a Whore*, IV, 1) is especially
fond of them:

> Ere I'd endure this sight, to see my love
> Clipt by another, I would dare confusion,
> And stand the horror of ten thousand deaths.

30. Marlowe, *2 Tamb.*, IV, 2.
31. Jonson, *Catiline*, V, 5.

And again (v, 3):

> Not go! stood death
> Threatening his armies of confounding plagues,
> With hosts of dangers hot as blazing stars,
> I would be there.

Even Shakespeare breaks loose in a similar manner
(*Coriolanus*, III, 3):

> Thou injurious tribune!
> Within thine eyes sat twenty thousand deaths,
> In thy hands clutch'd as many millions, in
> Thy lying tongue both numbers, I would say
> "Thou liest" unto thee.

But hyperbole, even if it is in the grand style, is
not the most significant thing about the Elizabethan
use of verbal conventions of death. What is suggestive to the student of literature is the relation between the background of convention and the awaken-
ing of that convention into fresh poetic vitality. And
in order to see this revivifying process at work, and
to give point to our remarks, let us trace the history
of one more image and see what happened to it in
Elizabethan drama.

The reader has probably observed that in several
of the quotations given in the first two chapters the
human body, or human life as a whole, has been
compared to a prison. The comparison first appears
in Greece as part of the Orphic doctrine, which
taught that the divine soul of man was imprisoned
in the body as a tomb; the expression is first used by
Plato (*supra*, p. 5). After Plato it became very
common, for it exactly fitted the popular ideas of

which Orphism was only one manifestation. Cicero used it in his *De Senectute*: "Indeed, while we are shut up in this *prison* of the body, we are performing a heavy task laid upon us by necessity." [32] It is, in fact, always employed by those who believe that the soul is not at home in the world, but belongs elsewhere, whence it has been sent as a form of punishment. Our present life in the body is death, says Philo Judaeus, for the body is the "utterly polluted prison" of the soul.[33]

Naturally, therefore, when Orphism, Platonism, asceticism, and the intellectual twilight which began to settle down over civilized Europe in the second century had combined to ensure the success of Christianity, that religion, in its turn, regarded the body as a prison. In the Middle Ages the phrase occurs again and again, in the plays of Hrotsvitha,[34] in two of the treatises on the art of dying,[35] in Petrarch,[36] and in Chaucer.[37]

32. Trans. A. P. Peabody, Boston, 1912, XXI.

33. *De Migr. Abr.*, II; Mangey, II, 437. Quoted in R. H. Charles, *Critical History of the Doctrine of a Future Life*, etc., London, 1899, p. 260.

34. *Dulcitius*, sc. XI, trans. C. St. John, London, 1923: "But we are weary of this world, and we implore Thee to break the *bonds* that *chain* our souls."

35. F. M. Comper, *The Book of the Craft of Dying*, London, 1917, first selection, chap. I: "Death is nothing else but a going out of *prison*, and an ending of exile."

36. Sonnetto LXXXVI (*in vita*):
   "Ma 'l sovrastar, nella *prigion* terrestra
      Cagion m'è, lasso, d'infiniti mali."

37. *Cant. Tales*, A 3061:

It is common enough, too, in sixteenth-century poetry. Barnaby Barnes speaks of the body as "that base *prison* of terrestiall rust," [38] and of the "bondage of this *prison* foule." [39] "This body is a *gaole*," says Thomas Storer.[40] Bartholomew Griffin uses the notion in his sonnets to Fidessa:

> my soul . . .
> That is *imprisoned* in a lump of clay,[41]

and there at least seven other uses of it in sixteenth-century poetry.[42] It is one of the commonest and most ancient of all the expressions connected with death, and it was always repeated in the same way. Before we come to the drama, Nashe is the only person I am acquainted with who gives the phrase a new turn. Our clothes, he says, "are a second flesh-assisting *prison*, and further corrupting weight of

---

"That good Arcite . . .
    Departed is . . .
    Out of this foule *prison* of this lyf."

38. "Divine Centurie of Spiritual Sonnets" (1595), son. XLIX; in *Heliconia, ed. cit.*, vol. II.

39. *Ibid.*, son. LXXXXI.

40. "Life and Death of Thomas Wolsey," in *Heliconia, ed. cit.*, II, 78.

41. "Fidessa," in *Elizabethan Sonnet Cycles*, ed. M. F. Crowe, London, 1897, III, son. XXVIII.

42. Alexander Hume, *Poems*, ed. A. Lawson, Scottish Text Soc. (Edinburgh, 1902), p. 35:

Thow hes not yet bein threttie yeirs and ane,
Into this fleshlie *prison* resident.

Rowlands, *Battel betweene Time and Death, ed. cit.*, p. 27:

The *prison* of man's soule thou canst not breake.

corruption cast on our soules to keepe them from soaring to heaven." [43]

Even the drama used it, for the most part, in a commonplace manner. Kyd opens the *Spanish Tragedy* with it:

> When this eternal substance of my soul
> Did live *imprison'd* in my wanton flesh;

Massinger employs it in *The Roman Actor* (IV, 2):

> His soul is freed
> From the *prison* of his flesh; let it mount upward;

Shakespeare repeats it in *King John* (III, 4):

> Look, who comes here! a grave unto a soul;
> Holding the eternal spirit, against her will,
> In the vile *prison* of afflicted breath;

and it is used in *Nero* (IV, 6):

> Thou loathly this *imprisoning* flesh put'st on.

The metaphor in these quotations is still expressed thoughtlessly, with no internal conviction, with no intellectual or emotional realization of what the word implies.

William Loe, "Poems," in *Miscellanies of the Fuller Worthies' Library*, ed. Grossart (London, 1871), I, 488:
> Death is the judge to quitt from *jayle*.

Henry Lok, "Poems," *ibid.*, II, 151:
> The body is the *prison* where it [the soul] readie is to pine.

Ibid., II, 206: "Bodie's *prison*."

R. Devereux, Second Earl of Essex, *ibid.*, IV, 447:
> Welcome sweet Death . . . this fleshly *prison* of my soule unlocke.

43. "Christs Teares" in *Works*, ed. R. B. McKerrow, London, 1910, II, 142.

But then something happened, and after the phrase had been repeated countless times for two thousand years by Greek, Jew, and Christian, it suddenly took on a new form. Webster for the first time revitalized it and grasped its meaning in all its connotations:

Thou art a box of worm-seed, at best but a salvatory of green mummy. What's this flesh? A little crudded milk, fantastical puff-paste. Out bodies are weaker than those paper-prisons boys use to keep flies in; more contemptible, since ours is to preserve earth-worms. Didst thou ever see a lark in a cage? Such is the soul in the body: this world is like her little turf of grass, and the heaven o'er our heads, like her looking-glass, only gives us a miserable knowledge of the small compass of our prison (*Duchess of Malfi*, IV, 2).

This process of the revitalization of old phrases is perhaps the most striking fact to be noticed in studying the Elizabethan verbal treatment of death. But it is dependent on a second fact which I trust our study has adequately illustrated: the extreme communality of the words and phrases which were capable of being revitalized. There was a collection of established remarks about death formed by tradition and waiting for anybody's use; the more one reads the plays, the more similarities one finds. Shakespeare's "Out, out, brief candle," for example, strikes us as an original and effective phrase. Effective it is, but it is not original.

> What booteth it to live in base contempt . . .
> *Out with thy candle*, let it burne no more,

says Anthony Copley (1596).[44] Clifford exclaims
(*3 Henry VI*, II, 6), when wounded to the death:
"Here burns my *candle* out." The King James
Bible has: "His *candle* shall be put out with him"
(*Job*, XVIII, 6). And Fletcher's Ordella (*Thierry and Theodoret*, IV, 1) says:

> . . . Those are . . . mad that stay it [death],
> Till age blow out their lights.

Without this common background, of course, —
the contrast between light and darkness, between
life and death — Shakespeare's phrase would lose
its power, just as without the revitalization that
Shakespeare gives it, the phrase would, like the remarks of Dekker's Duke, be only another "sentence." We can find this fact exemplified again and
again. I quote a passage from *King John* (III, 4)
which includes more remarks about death than any
other I am acquainted with. Queen Constance is
speaking:

> Death, death: O, amiable lovely death!
> Thou odoriferous stench! sound rottenness!
> Arise forth from the couch of lasting night,
> Thou hate and terror to prosperity,
> And I will kiss thy detestable bones,
> And put my eyeballs in thy vaulty brows,
> And ring these fingers with thy household worms,
> And stop this gap of breath with fulsome dust,
> And be a carrion monster like thyself:

---

44. *A Fig For Fortune*, ed. Spenser Society (1883), p. 12.

Come, grin on me; and I will think thou smil'st
And buss thee as thy wife! Misery's love,
O! come to me.

Here there is not a single remark we have not heard before. We have seen how death is sweet or amiable to those in distress; the emphasis on putrefaction was very common in the Middle Ages; we know that death is associated with night, that it destroys worldly things in a hateful and terrible way, that it is bony, eyeless, and results in worms and dust; we know that death is a monster, that he grins (as in the Dances of Death), that people greet him as a bridegroom. From one point of view the passage is a patchwork of platitudes, and one could almost imagine that Shakespeare was here consciously making a collection of them; at least Constance's speech illustrates how ready such platitudes lay to hand. But the paradoxical juxtapositions, the new order in which the old phrases are arranged, the new adjectives ("vaulty," "household," "fulsome") attached to the familiar nouns, the mounting, rhetorical rhythm — all these things show how platitudes can be made into successful poetry.

Yet lacking the background of platitude, the poetry would be impossible. If our study of the Elizabethan vocabulary about death has shown us nothing else, it has shown the necessity for a common understanding, a common basis of convention, between the poet and his audience. Without this common basis, the suggestiveness and terror of Romeo's speech about the "lean abhorred monster," to choose only one example out of a thousand, would be non-existent; both the poet and his audience must have the image of the skeleton sharply before them. We might even go further and state that granted the poet's native gifts, the more rooted in convention he is, the more *imaginative* his writing will be. The imaginative insight of a poet is most effective and most moving when his subject-matter is most universal, and if he can at the same time make use of a familiar vocabulary, a set of generally accepted images, and awaken them to new poetic life, then his writing will be all the more successful. One of the reasons why, to anyone who knows medieval literature, St. Bernard's prayer to the Virgin in the last canto of Dante's *Paradiso* is so moving is that it is filled with phrases that had been employed over and over again by poets who had previously written of the Virgin, and our pleasure comes almost as much from our recognition of their familiarity as it does from our delight and wonder at the new perfection with which they are used. It is, in fact, an error in analysis to separate the two emotions; they are inextricably bound together.

The Elizabethans must have felt the same way when they heard such speeches as that of Constance about death. The images were familiar, but the arrangement and the precise expression were new.

We might say that the proper use of conventional images in poetry is similar to the proper use of a metrical pattern. Our pleasure in good blank verse is derived from our awareness of a familiar and regular beat combined with our recognition of conflicting rhythms conditioned by the meaning; so, when we read successful poetry about a universal subject such as death, we are pleased both by the familiarity of the images and the new applications which the poet gives them.

But these new applications must be made with tact, and it goes almost without saying that they will not be successful unless the poet manages to persuade us that they are filled with the weight of a convincing emotion. We can see very clearly the difference between an effective and an ineffective use of conventional imagery if we compare Webster's description of life as a prison (p. 103) with Shirley's account of death as a bridegroom (p. 77). Shirley tries to surprise us: he does not reveal his simile until he has given a list of supposedly tantalizing and anticipatory details; our curiosity, our nerves, are excited, and we have to wait until he is prepared to satisfy us with the conclusion we have already half anticipated. But Webster fills us from the beginning. We have here no rhetorical pauses, no list of sentimental details to beguile us toward the melodramatic conclusion; all is open and fair — the image is given to us at once, and we do not get nervous waiting for it to surprise us at the end. Shirley writes as if he were outside his subject, but Webster and his subject are one, with the result that we have in the rhythm of his magnificent prose a weight and an authority that the languorous and sentimental blank verse of Shirley entirely lacks.

It is also true that when a poet is writing about a matter which has a number of conventional images attached to it, such as death, he cannot afford to neglect those images and substitute others of his own. If he does so, his writing at once loses its richness and its vigor; it becomes thin and artificial. This is a danger the Elizabethans seem to have avoided. They very rarely, if ever, use a simile or an adjective about death which is irrelevant to the general body of association. But the later poets of the seventeenth century were not so careful: in trying to be clever they overstepped the bounds of convention, and instead of being imaginative, to use Coleridge's distinction, they became merely fanciful. I know of no better illustration of this fact than the last stanza of Dryden's "Ode on the Memory of Mrs. Killigrew":

When in mid-air the golden trump shall sound
   To raise the nations under ground;
   When in the Valley of Jehosaphat
The judging God shall close the book of fate,
   And there the last assizes keep
   For those who wake and those who sleep;

> When rattling bones together fly
> From the four corners of the sky;
> When sinews o'er the skeletons are spread,
> Those cloth'd with flesh, and life inspires the dead;
> The sacred poets first shall hear the sound,
> And foremost from the tomb shall bound,
> For they are cover'd with the lightest ground;
> And straight, with inborn vigor, on the wing,
> Like mounting larks to the new morning sing.
> There thou, sweet saint, before the choir shalt go,
> As harbinger of heav'n, the way to show,
> The way which thou so well hast learn'd below.

The stanza begins splendidly, with a highly imaginative picture of the Last Judgment, based, be it noticed, on all the *conventional* details, firmly established in the reader's mind by tradition, but given a fresh and admirable expression. Dryden is here at his imaginative best, and we are exalted by it. But at the crucial point he intrudes his own conception, and at once we are on a lower level:

> The sacred poets first shall hear the sound,
> And leaping from their tombs shall bound, etc.

No one, as far as I know, had ever suggested before that the first people to rise at the Last Judgment might be the poets; the idea is a conceit, a private invention, and after the opening lines it is an anti-climax. It comes as a *surprise*, not as a *satisfaction*, and it is not welcomed, as were the images of the first lines, by a set of associations in the reader's mind, which spring to new life at the poet's words.

I emphasize this point, though it is outside the main line of our discussion, for it is one of the most valuable for the study of poetry that our remarks about the Elizabethan vocabulary have raised. It would suggest that convention is essential for imaginative writing, and that imaginative writing is likely to flourish best in a period when a number of vivid conventional images about important subjects are present. The suggestion has implications which extend far beyond Elizabethan drama.

Chapter IV

THE ELIZABETHAN DRAMA: IDEAS

As one had been a mirror to another,
Like forms of life and death, each took from other;
And so were life and death mix'd at their heights,
That you could see no fear of death, for life,
Nor love of life, for death.

Chapman, *Bussy D'Ambois*

I

TO separate the Elizabethan ideas of death from their verbal expression is not an easy, nor in the long run a legitimate, task. The thought and the words form a single poetic whole, which cannot be completely defined by a description of its parts. But for our study of the Elizabethan mind and emotions, the separation, if arbitrary, is essential; though the new organizations of words would not have existed without the new organizations of thought, and the thought would have been stillborn without the words, nevertheless, from the historical point of view, the words and the thought must be treated as two things. The fire must be described apart from the coal which it burns, and the coal which is burnt must be analyzed separately from the flame it creates. Only by so doing can we understand the richness and the significance of the Elizabethan dramatic treatment of death.

The most obvious of all the ideas connected with death is that it is universal:

> it is the inevitable fate
> Of all things underneath the moon.

In Elizabethan times the thought had its own phrase, "We all must die," which was often repeated. Dekker's Duke, uses it (*1 Honest Whore*, 1, 3):

> Nay do not weep for him; we all must die;

Aëcius, in Fletcher's *Valentinian* (IV, 4) adopts it to comfort his friends before he dies: "And must we leave you, sir?" they inquire; and Aëcius replies: "We must all die; All leave ourselves." "I know, uncle, We must all die," says little Hengo in the same author's *Bonduca* (IV, 2). Shakespeare uses the remark twice: once (*Julius Caesar*, IV, 3) when Brutus hears of Portia's death:

> Why, farewell, Portia. We must die, Messala:
> With meditating that she must die once,
> I have the patience to endure it now;

again (*Hamlet*, I, 2), when the Queen, seeking to stop Hamlet's mourning, says:

> Thou know'st 'tis common; all that live must die,
> Passing through nature to eternity.
> *Hamlet:* Ay, madam, it is common.

In both these cases the phrase is recognized as a platitude. Brutus utters it in order to give an impression of carelessness he does not feel (the rhythm of the line seems to establish that), and the Queen speaks it so that we may realize the shallowness of her nature. Shakespeare (and Dekker too for that matter) is fully conscious of the flatness of the remark, and uses it for purposes of character drawing. It is put in its correct emotional and psychological atmosphere.

Shakespeare does the same thing with another opinion, which, like this one, had become paralyzed in a platitude: "Death is [the] end of all," a phrase which Florio insipidly uses to translate Horace's "mors ultima linea rerum est." [1] When in *Romeo and Juliet* Tybalt is killed, Shakespeare is anxious to avoid arousing any emotion over him; he wants to save it for his chief characters. Consequently the nurse (III, 3) speaks of Tybalt's death as follows: "Well, death's the end of all"; and Capulet, a scene later, says, "Well, we were born to die" — two observations so trite, and so slightingly expressed, as to have no emotional value whatever. The audience is expected to take its cue from the speakers, and show equally little feeling.

We have observed frequently enough that the Middle Ages looked on the present world as vile, and the opinion was commonly repeated in the sixteenth century. Naturally we find it again in Elizabethan literature; our recent discussion of the body in terms of a prison has already given an example of

1. Montaigne, i, 19.

it. And just as that particular aspect of the Christian attitude towards life had its own phrase, so the more general notion of the world's rottenness was trapped in word or two, and frozen there. It is instructive to observe Shakespeare's use of it:

> No longer mourn for me when I am dead
> Than you shall hear the surly sullen bell
> Give warning to the world that I am fled
> From *this vile world*, with vilest worms to dwell.
>
> (Son. LXXI)

The adjective "vile" is here not used quite seriously: its conventionality and flatness are recognized, and turned to advantage. No weightiness is aimed at, but an intermediate effect, half-way between weariness and intensity, like a sigh. Only Shakespeare was sufficiently sensitive to conventional expressions to be able to use them so subtly.

Cleopatra expresses the same idea in a more personal way, which is excellently suited to her character and situation (*Antony and Cleopatra*, IV, 13):

> Shall I abide
> In this dull world, which in thy absence is
> No better than a sty?

But usually the thought was stated less vigorously. One of the characters in *Gorboduc*, as we know, merely calls life "loathsome"; and Arostus (in the same play), who has the reputation of wisdom, only repeats a series of stock remarks, like Chaucer's Egeus, to justify it:

Your Grace should now in these grave years of yours
Have found ere this the price of mortal joys:
How short they be, how fading here in earth,
How full of change, how brittle our estate.

(IV, 2)

The Duke in *Measure for Measure*, however, when talking on this matter, even though his subject is stale, transforms it entirely (III, 1):

Be absolute for death; either death or life
Shall thereby be the sweeter. Reason thus with life:
If I do lose thee, I do lose a thing
That none but fools would keep: a breath thou art,
Servile to all the skyey influences,
That dost this habitation, where thou keep'st,
Hourly afflict,

and on for many lines:

Thy best of rest is sleep,
And that thou oft provok'st; yet grossly fear'st
Thy death, which is no more.

The idea is familiar to us; but again, as so often before, the new language with which it is expressed gives it force. Indeed Claudio, to whom the Duke is lecturing, is converted, as after such a speech he was almost bound to be:

I humbly thank you,
To sue to live, I find I seek to die,
And, seeking death, find life: let it come on.

Marston, like Shakespeare, magnifies the old conception (*Malcontent*, IV, 2):

Think this: — this earth is the only grave and Golgotha wherein all things that live must rot; 'tis but the draught wherein the heavenly bodies discharge their corruption; the very muck-hill on which the sublunary orbs cast their excrements.

It is worth observing that Malevole, who speaks these lines, is trying to persuade the regent Pietro to give up worldly things. And, like Shakespeare's Duke, he succeeds. Pietro remarks, almost immediately afterwards:

> In true contrition, I do dedicate
> My breath to solitary holiness.

Both Shakespeare and Marston, that is, no matter in how Elizabethan a fashion they may express it, use the old medieval idea in a medieval way: in order that men's thoughts may be turned from the world. They use it consciously for dramatic purposes; hence we cannot say that they accepted it, as they accepted so many words and phrases their ancestors had passed on to them, without thinking. The notion had, even to them, a definitely religious and medieval connotation, and it was deliberately used in this connotation alone. Indeed it would never have come to life at all, as it so splendidly did, if it had been accepted thoughtlessly.

Expression of the belief in immortality naturally occurs with considerable frequency in the plays. Queen Elizabeth (*Richard III*, II, 2) urges the Duchess to die quickly:

> That our swift-winged souls may catch the king's;
> Or, like obedient subjects, follow him,
> To his new kingdom of perpetual rest.

So Isabella, in Marston's play *The Insatiate Countess* (v, 1), in spite of her lecherous life dies in confidence of heaven:

> Murder and lust, down with my ashes sink,
> But, like ingrateful seed, perish in earth,
> That you may never spring against my soul,
> Like weeds to choke it in the heavenly harvest.
> I fall to rise; mount to thy Maker, spirit!

As a consequence of this faith in a next world one of the favorite speeches to put in the mouth of a dying character was an expression of confidence that he would meet his loved ones there. Queen Elizabeth, as we have just observed, is confident that she and her children will meet their king in heaven. Clermont D'Ambois (*The Revenge of Bussy D'Ambois*, v, 5) exclaims to the imagined Guise:

> I come, my lord! Clermont, thy creature, comes.

And the dying Aëcius in Fletcher's *Valentinian* (IV, 4) cries:

> I come, ye blessèd spirits; make me room
> To live for ever in Elysium!

But there was another side to the picture: the medieval emphasis on hell bore ample fruit in the drama. *Faustus* is one of the best examples of the way it was used, even though Mephistophilis' definition of hell has a broader sweep than anything of the kind in the Middle Ages:

> Why this is hell, nor am I out of it (sc. 3).

For Faustus himself, in his last agonized moments, has a literal image burning before him, when the familiar horrors rise again in all their malignancy:

> My God! my God! look not so fierce on me!
> Adders and serpents, let me breathe awhile!
> Ugly hell, gape not! come not, Lucifer!
> I'll burn my books!

In *Tamburlaine* (pt. 2, II, 3), Marlowe uses a description of hell to give a very sudden and startling effect. Sigismund dies, like many of his dramatic contemporaries, with a hopeful piety:

> And let this death, wherein to sin I die,
> Conceive a second life in endless mercy!

But his enemy Orcanes, standing over him, produces a striking contrast by declaring Sigismund's certainty of hell:

> Now scalds his soul in the Tartarian streams,
> And feeds upon the baneful tree of hell,
> That Zoacum, that fruit of bitterness
> That in the midst of fire is ingraffed,
> Yet flourisheth as Flora in her pride,
> With apples like the heads of damned fiends,
> The devils there, in chains of quenchless flame
> Shall lead his soul through Orcus' burning gulf,
> From pain to pain, whose change shall never end.[2]

---

2. This passage is a curious mixture of three religions. Tartarus, of course, is classical, and the devils who lead the soul through pains are probably Christian, though the fact that these pains are continually changing is foreign to the orthodox Christian hell, where each sinner's punishment remains eternally the same. The account sounds much more like Owayn's tour of Purgatory, though

This speech, however, effective as it is, does not contribute to the development of plot or character: it neither foreshadows events to come, nor brings about a conversion. But the later dramatists soon became aware of how useful, for such dramatic purposes, a description of hell could be. This is particularly true of Shakespeare. His earliest account of hell is in *Richard III* (I, 4), where Clarence, in superb language, describes his dream to Brakenbury:

> I pass'd, methought, the melancholy flood,
> With that grim ferryman which poets write of,
> Unto the kingdom of perpetual night.
> The first that there did greet my stranger soul,
> Was my great father-in-law, renowned Warwick;
> Who cried aloud, "What scourge for perjury
> Can this dark monarchy afford false Clarence?"
> And so he vanish'd: then came wandering by
> A shadow like an angel, with bright hair
> Dabbled in blood; and he shriek'd out aloud,

---

doubtless there is no direct connection. The description of the tree, and its fruit, Zoacum, is from the Koran, sura 37, vv. 60 ff. (Rodwell's translation): "The tree Ez-zakkourm. . . . It is a tree which cometh up from the bottom of hell; Its fruit is as it were the heads of Satans; And lo! the damned shall surely eat of it and fill their bellies with it." Marlowe again describes hell in *1 Tamb.*, v, 2: Zabina says that the "infamous, monstrous slaveries" of Tamburlaine are worse than hell:

> Gape, earth, and let the fiends infernal view
> A hell as hopeless and as full of fear
> As are the blasted banks of Erebus,
> Where shaking ghosts with ever howling groans
> Hover about the ugly ferryman,
> To get a passage to Elysium

— a description predominantly classical, though its fear and ever-howling groans sound like a medieval addition.

"Clarence is come, — false, fleeting, perjur'd Clarence,
That stabb'd me in the field by Tewksbury; —
Seize on him! Furies, take him into torment."
With that, methought, a legion of foul fiends
Environ'd me, and howled in mine ears
Such hideous cries, that with the very noise
I trembling wak'd, and, for a season after,
Could not believe but that I was in hell,
Such terrible impression made my dream.

Here, as in Marlowe, the classical and medieval notions of hell are mixed. Styx, Charon, and the
Furies are side by side with foul fiends who make
hideous cries.[3] But this is to be expected, and occurs
in nearly all Elizabethan descriptions of hell.[4] The

3. See Chaucer, *Cant. Tales*, B 4579: "They yelleden as feendes
doon in helle." This was a very common medieval belief — one
can find many expressions of it.

4. Somewhat similar to the use of classical names and descriptions of hell is the use of classical symbols for death. Atropos and
her thread-cutting are often a synonym for decease. The earliest
reference to her that I am aware of in English poetry is in Lydgate,
Troy Book, II, 4694 ff., when Lydgate laments Chaucer's decease:

Gret cause have I and mater to compleyne
On *Antropos* and up-on hir envie,
That brak the threde and made for to dye
Noble Galfride, poete of Breteyne.

After Lydgate's time it becomes fairly common. Sir David Lyndsay uses it in his "Secunde Epistyl of the Papyngo": "O *Atropus*,
warye we maye thy weird" and again in his *Monarche*, ed. E. E. T. S.
(1865), II, 338:

All men begynnis for tyll de
The day of thare Natavitie;
And Journelly they do proceid
Tyll Atropos cute the fatell threid.

The Mirror for Magistrates has it ("Brutus," st. 70):

Farewell, farewell, to mourne will not prevayle,
I see with knife where *Atropos* doth stand.

chief interest of this passage lies in its dramatic use. Clarence's dream forms a very dramatic prelude to the murder which occurs in the following scene; and the audience, accustomed to omens and premonitions, as it was accustomed, both by belief and dramatic practice, to ghosts, must have waited with heightened expectation to see the almost certain fulfilment of Clarence's gloomy forebodings.

In *Hamlet* (I, 5) the ghost's suggestive hints about purgatorial torture (the use of purgatory instead of hell shows how easy it was for Shakespeare to use an old-fashioned but still vivid belief for the sake of greater dramatic plausibility) — these hints are also employed dramatically, though for a different purpose than Clarence's dream. Shakespeare wants to have the audience pay as close attention as possible to what is to follow; old Hamlet's account of his murder is of the greatest importance for the understanding of the plot. So, just as at the beginning of the play the audience is caught at once by the darkness, the crisp words of the guards, and the general air of mystery, the atmosphere of horror here created by the ghost enforces attention:

> But that I am forbid
> To tell the secrets of my prison-house,

But it does not seem to have occurred much in the drama; the more vivid figure of death himself, being far closer to the audience's knowledge and experience, was more effective than such a purely literary allusion.

> I could a tale unfold whose lightest word
> Would harrow up thy soul, freeze thy young blood,
> Make thy two eyes, like stars, start from their spheres,
> Thy knotted and combined locks to part,
> And each particular hair to stand on end,
> Like quills upon the fretful porpentine:
> But this eternal blazon must not be
> To ears of flesh and blood. List, list, O list. . . .

There is no literal description — it is all suggestion. But unless the audience had had behind it the long tradition of punishment after death, emphasized by Catholic and Calvinist, this suggestion would not have been effective. It is a further example of the dependence of the dramatist upon popular conviction.

In *Measure for Measure* the thought of future punishment is used for still another purpose: to exhibit character. Claudio, overcome by the dread of something after death, imagines the tortures of the other life:

> To be imprison'd in the viewless winds
> And blown with restless violence round about
> The pendant world; or to be worse than worst
> Of those that lawless and incertain thoughts
> Imagine howling: 'tis too horrible!

This appalling vision so frightens him that he decides not to give his life for his sister's chastity. His fear of the terrors of hell, contrary to its desired effect in the Middle Ages, turns him back to this world, and he forgets the willingness to die which he had expressed only a few minutes before. His acceptance of the Duke's medieval sermon had been superficial, and his subsequent rebellion against it not only illustrates his character, but has a significance, as we shall see later, in the history of Elizabethan emotion as a whole.

Thus Shakespeare makes the old tradition of future punishment useful for creating character, atmosphere, and plot. And Shakespeare's triple employment of it gives the key to its use by the other dramatists. D'Amville, in the *Atheist's Tragedy* (IV, 3), being on the point of distraction owing to the result of his atheistical convictions, at once succumbs to the belief he had affected to despise. When the watch enters, he imagines, in his fright, that they are infernal agents:

> Black Beelzebub,
> And all his hell-hounds, come to apprehend me?

a remark which reveals how shallow his atheism is — and in that shows his character. But it is not nearly so revealing of D'Amville's character as it is of Tourneur's. To the Elizabethans an atheist was a creature viewed with superstitious horror, and it was only natural that when such a person began to lose his self-confidence, he should see the blackest of medieval devils waiting to snatch him.

Middleton uses hell in a somewhat similar fashion, in connection with lust. Beatrice and DeFlores have been caught in their adulterous proceedings; to their discoverer, Alsemero, as to Middleton's audience, they are certain to pay for it in hell. And Alsemero, thrusting the pair into a closet, urges them on with that violent and bitter irony so frequent in late Elizabethan drama:

> Rehearse again
> Your scene of lust, that you may be perfect
> When you shall come to act it to the black audience,
> Where howls and gnashings shall be music to you.
> Clip your adulteress freely, 'tis the pilot
> Will guide you to the *mare mortuum*,
> Where you shall sink to fathoms bottomless.
>
> (*Changeling*, v, 38)

But it is Ford who uses the idea of hell most dramatically, at the same time describing it in the most medieval imagery. In *'Tis Pity She's a Whore*, Annabella and her brother have committed incest; Annabella sits alone in her chamber weeping at the thought of what she has done, when a friar comes to see her (iii, 6):

> These tears may do you good; weep faster yet
> Whilst I do read a lecture.

This he proceeds most vividly to do.

> Ay, you are wretched, miserably wretched,
> Almost condemn'd alive. There is a place,
> List, daughter! in a black and hollow vault,
> Where day is never seen; there shines no sun,
> But flaming horror of consuming fires,
> A lightless sulphur, chok'd with smoky fogs
> Of an infected darkness: in this place

> Dwell many thousand thousand sundry sorts
> Of never-dying deaths: there damned souls
> Roar without pity; there are gluttons fed
> With toads and adders; there is burning oil
> Poured down the drunkard's throat; the usurer
> Is forced to sup whole draughts of molten gold;
> There is the murderer forever stabb'd,
> Yet can he never die; there lies the wanton
> On racks of burning steel, whilst in his soul
> He feels the torment of his raging lust.

Ann: Mercy! Oh mercy!

Friar: There stand these wretched things,
> Who have dream'd out whole years on lawless sheets
> And secret incests, cursing one another:
> Then you will wish each kiss your brother gave,
> Had been a dagger's point; then you shall hear
> How he will cry, "Oh, would my wicked sister
> Had first been damn'd, when she did yield to lust!" —
> But soft, methinks I see repentance work
> New motions in your heart; say, how is't with you?

Hell here comes to the stage with all its medieval fury. Even the particular torment for the particular sin is repeated, as the most effective means for frightening; and, as in *Richard III*, the vividness of the description is intensified by having the character see himself among the damned. This scene is also the turning point of the play; the friar entirely converts Annabella, and she, by following the advice he gives her after he has broken down her resistance, helps to produce the tragic conclusion. The doctrine which Pope Innocent III had expressed in his *De Contemptu Mundi* is used as a substitute for the recognition scene of Aristotle, and Ford's employment of it shows how thoroughly it was embedded in the popular mind. The spectators of a play have to be convinced of the reality of both the actual and the psychological changes that take place before them, and only by the fact that the preachers of the Middle Ages, and their descendants in Elizabethan times, had used hell just as Ford used it — to cause fear and repentance — were they in a position to be convinced of the reality of Annabella's conversion.[5]

The classical picture of the other-world was, of course, in the mind of the audience too, and the way in which classical and medieval details were

5. Hell was not always used seriously in the drama. There are at least two plays where, after the fashion of the medieval poems about Cockaigne, fun is made of the other world. One of these is Greene's *Friar Bacon and Friar Bungay* (sc. 15):

Miles: But I pray you, sir, do you come lately from hell?

Devil: Ay marry: how then?

Miles: Faith, 'tis a place I have desired long to see. Have you not good tippling-houses there? May not a man have a lusty fire there, a pot of good ale, a pair of cards, a swinging piece of chalk, and a brown toast that will clap a white waistcoat on a cup of good drink?

Devil: All this you may have there.

And Flamineo in Webster's *White Devil* (v, 6) speaks as follows: "O Lucian, thy ridiculous purgatory! to find Alexander the Great cobbling shoes, Pompey tagging points, and Julius Caesar making hair-buttons! Hannibal selling blacking, and Augustus crying garlic! Charlemagne selling lists by the dozen, and King Pepin crying apples in a cart drawn with one horse!" For Lucian's Purgatory, see his *Menippus*; but Webster's characters, though their occupations are much the same, have different names than Lucian's. Flamineo in this speech makes fun of hell very effectively, for though he is *apparently* about to die, yet he knows that he is not, and his mockery is highly appropriate.

mingled or separated by the dramatists is a matter
of some interest. Though the two traditions, as we
have seen, often occur in the same passage, the
Elizabethans, on the whole, were careful not to
make historical mistakes, and they kept Christian
details out of the way when a play had a classical
subject. Shakespeare exemplifies this clearly; I believe he never mentions any but classical images
when he refers to the other-world in his Roman
plays; Antony, for example, as he is dying (IV, 12)
thinks only of the Elysian fields:

> Where souls do couch on flowers, we'll hand in hand
> And with our sprightly port make the ghosts gaze;
> Dido and her Aeneas shall want troops,
> And all the haunt be ours.

If there was to be an anachronism, it was more
likely to be the other way about, and a classical
other-world would be spoken of in a play with a
Christian background. Literary fashion had a good
deal to do with this, and the anachronism was much
more common in the plays of the 'nineties than
later. Kyd begins his *Spanish Tragedy* with a rather
heavy-handed description of the stock figures in
Hades — Charon, Minos, and Rhadamanthus —
and Greene makes his characters in *Alphonsus* continually swear, like Tamburlaine, by pagan gods.
But in *Alphonsus* there is one illuminating passage
which helps to explain why, as the drama improved,
classical references grew rarer. Greene wants one of

his people, Belinus (II, 1), to express anger, and he
has him cry:

> What, is he gone? the devil break his neck,
> The fiends of hell torment his traitorous corpse!

The moment emotion enters in, the smart classical
references are forgotten and the more native, less
superficial, associations are called up. So, when the
drama as a whole became more expert in describing emotion, the picture of the other-world created
by the vital force of religion took the place of details
which were merely learned decorations; the result is
the dream of Clarence and the conversion of Annabella. At the end of our period even a careful writer
like the author of *Nero* (printed 1624) was more
ready to put Christian references into the mouth of a
Roman character than were his predecessors, and
we get passages like this (III, 6):

> Nero, this day must end the world's desires,
> And headlong send thee to unquenchèd fires.

The picture called up in the mind of the audience
was undoubtedly not the fire of Phlegethon, but the
fire of the Christian hell.

But immortality was to be found not only in the
other world. We have seen that in the Renaissance
the desire for earthly fame, though other-worldly
teaching opposed it, was expressed, in all kinds of
writing, as if it were as much a part of established
belief as its exact opposite. Webster, for example,

wrote in his dedication of the *Duchess of Malfi* to Lord Berkeley:

by such Poems as this, Poets have kissed the hands of Great Princes, and drawn their gentle eyes to look down upon their sheets of paper, when the Poets themselves were bound up in their winding-sheets. The like courtesy from your Lordship, shall make you live in your grave, and laurel spring out of it; when the ignorant scorners of the Muses . . . shall wither, neglected, and forgotten.

The desire for worldly immortality took the same forms in Elizabethan popular literature that it had taken in Greece. Plato had mentioned children, good deeds, and writings as ways of making one's name remain after death; [6] these recur in Elizabethan times. Immortality through descendants is referred to by Marlowe and Tourneur; [7] in dedications and lyrical poems the immortality of the poet is assured; but it was upon the eternity of the fame produced by good deeds that most emphasis was laid in the plays. Just as reputation,

> fame's dear life
> Which is above life,[8]

---

6. *Symposium*, 209.
7. *2 Tamb.*, v, 3 (Tamburlaine is addressing his sons):
> My flesh, divided in your precious shapes
> Shall still retain my spirit, though I die,
> And live in all your seeds immortally.

Atheist's Tragedy, v, 1 (D'Amville's sons have both died):
> *D'Amville:* Can nature be
>   So simple or malicious to destroy
>   The reputation of her proper memory?

8. Chapman, *Bussy D'Ambois*, ii, 1.

was of paramount importance in this world, so it was essential that the memory of one's good deeds should remain after one had left it. The very fact that they *were* good was sometimes an automatic assurance of immortality. Marston's Sophonisba exclaims:

> O my stars,
> I bless your goodness, that with breast unstain'd,
> Faith pure, a virgin wife, tried to my glory,
> I die, of female faith the long-lived story.
>
> (*Sophonisba*, v, 38)

And she was not the only one who, "tried to her glory" and following the long tradition of Roman virgins and Christian saints, expired with a confidence that her fame was secure. Seneca remarks (*Nero*, IV, 6):

> Death from me nothing takes but what's a burthen,
> A clog to that free spark of heavenly fire;
> But that in Seneca the which you loved,
> Which you admired, doth and shall still remain,
> Secure of death, untouchèd of the grave.

According to Dekker (*1 Honest Whore*, IV, 1) it is good deeds which

> keep men sweet, long above ground.

His Orlando Friscobaldo (*2 Honest Whore*, I, 2) also remarks: "I would not die like a rich man, to carry nothing away save a winding sheet: but like a good man, to leave Orlando behind me": that is, the reputation of his good deeds. The sentiment may be found again and again.

> Integrity of life is fame's best friend,
> Which nobly, beyond death, shall crown the end,

says Delio in the *Duchess of Malfi* (v, 5), putting his words into a couplet, like most Elizabethan moralists. The careful Captain Ager, in Middleton's *Fair Quarrel* (ii, 1), when trying to make up his mind what to do after his mother has been called a whore, soliloquizes thus:

> I am too full of conscience . . .
> So careful of my eternity, which consists
> Of upright actions, that unless I knew
> It were a truth I stood for, any coward
> Might make my breast his foot-piece.

And his scrupulosity makes the subsequent action possible. We find the following couplet at the end of Marston's *Insatiate Countess*:

> Since man's best of life is fame,
> He hath need preserve the same.

The notion was common,[9] and, as this last quotation shows, it was often thoughtlessly and flatly repeated. Shakespeare's use of it, like all his uses of convention, is illuminating; no one was more aware than he of the tones of emotional hollowness or depth to

9. See also Massinger, *Roman Actor*, iv, 2:
   Alas! I know that the denial's death;
   Nor can my grant, discovered, threaten more.
   Yet to die innocent, and have the glory
   For all posterity to report that I

be struck by a sensitive employment of a conventional idea. In *Much Ado* (v, 3), Claudio reads from a scroll a formal lament for the supposedly dead Hero; he must say something appropriate, but at the same time he must not give the audience too strong an impression of grief, for if he did so it would be out of keeping with the tone of the play as a whole. Consequently he merely repeats, without any attempt to rejuvenate it, the convention of fame which we — like the Elizabethan audiences — already know so well:

> Done to death by slanderous tongues
> Was the Hero that here lies:
> Death, in guerdon of her wrongs,

> Refused an empress, to preserve my faith
> To my great master, in true judgment must
> Show fairer than to buy a guilty life
> With wealth and honours. 'Tis the base I build on.

Massinger, *Fatal Dowry*, IV, I:

> Season now your youth
> With one brave thing, and it shall keep the odor
> Even to your death, beyond, and on your tomb
> Scent like sweet oils and frankincense.

Chapman, *Bussy D'Ambois*, v, 4:

> Here like a Roman statue I will stand
> Till death hath made me marble. Oh, my fame,
> Live in despite of murther!

Titus Andronicus, I, I (referring to the family vault):

> Here none but soldiers and Rome's servitors
> Repose in fame.

Ibid.: He lives in fame that died in virtue's cause.

Coriolanus, v, 5:

> Beat thou the drum, that it speak mournfully. . . .
> Yet shall he have a noble memory.

> Gives her fame which never dies.
> So the life which died with shame
> Lives in death with glorious fame.

Once more we have an illustration of how valuable a convention can be to a dramatist who has the skill to use it properly.

In fact the use of this idea in the drama as a whole is revealing. The two strands of convention which lie behind it, the Christian emphasis on good deeds and the Renaissance emphasis on worldly immortality, are almost inextricably woven into a typical Elizabethan texture. Sometimes one is more obvious, sometimes the other, just as medieval and classical notions were continually shifting in every aspect of Elizabethan thought. But on the whole the Renaissance side of the argument had the better of it. Even though the Middle Ages had emphasized good deeds, it was not so much that the memory of them should remain on earth as that their performance might be useful for unlocking the gates of heaven. It was for this latter purpose that Everyman took his good deeds into the grave with him; he did not leave them, as Petrarch or an Elizabethan would have done, to keep his reputation alive on earth.[10]

Closely connected with the anxiety for remem-

10. Marston is an exception to, or perhaps a perverse illustration of, this general Elizabethan feeling. His *Scourge of Villainy* was dedicated to "Everlasting Oblivion," and he had the words "Oblivioni Sacrum" carved on his gravestone.

brance was a desire for a handsome funeral monument. Charles promises Joan of Arc (*1 Henry VI*,
1, 6):

> A statelier pyramis to her I'll rear
> Than Rhodope's or Memphis ever was:
> In memory of her when she is dead,
> Her ashes, in an urn more precious
> Than the rich-jewell'd coffer of Darius,
> Transported shall be at high festivals
> Before the kings and queens of France.

So Prince Edward (*Richard III*, III, 1), when he hears
how Caesar built the tower of London, says:

> Death makes no conquest of this conqueror
> For now he lives in fame, though not in life;

and Brutus, in Heywood's *Rape of Lucrece* (v, 6), is
given the following promise:

> O noble Brutus, this thy fame
> To after ages shall survive; thy body
> Shall have a fair and gorgeous sepulchre,
> For whom the matrons shall in funeral black
> Mourn twelve sad moons.[11]

The practice of raising monuments as a fortress
against oblivion was, however, criticized. Dekker
(*1 Honest Whore*, IV, 1) says:

> What fools are men to build a garish tomb,—
> Only to save the carcase whilst it rots,

---

11. See the dirge over "Fidele" in *Cymbeline*:
    Quiet consummation have;
    And renowned be thy grave.

> To maintain't long in stinking, make good carrion,
> But leave no good deeds to preserve them sound!
> For good deeds keep men sweet, long above ground,

a thought which brings us back to our previous convention.

As the reverse of this desire for a striking tomb, a private and nameless grave was the reward of the wicked, or the desire of only such a misanthrope as Timon. When Brunhalt, the vicious queen of Fletcher's *Thierry and Theodoret*, finally dies (v, 2) it is said of her,

> because
> She was born noble, let that title find her
> A private grave, but neither tongue nor honor.

The Elizabethans, in fact, seem to have dreaded nothing so much as the possibility that future generations might not know they had lived. Death had other horrible aspects, and their vivid imaginations, trained on the skeleton and the rest of the inherited teaching, did not fail to appreciate them, as we have seen. But the blankness of being forgotten was of all thoughts the most tormenting. This is well brought out by a scene in the *White Devil* (v, 3). Brachiano has been poisoned and lies in a half-conscious condition on a bed; Lodovico and Gasparo, his poisoners, enter dressed as Capuchin friars. They have come, they say, to give him the last rites of the Church, and on this pretence they are left alone with him. When the room is empty, they reveal themselves, and proceed to torture the dying man with every mental device they can think of. They leave the most cruel of their suggestions to the last:

> *Gasparo:* This is Count Lodovico.
> *Lodovico:* This, Gasparo:
> And thou shalt die like a poor rogue.
> *Gasparo:* And stink
> Like a dead fly-blown dog.
> *Lodovico:* And be forgotten
> Before thy funeral sermon.
> *Brachiano:* Vittoria!
> Vittoria!
> *Lodovico:* O, the cursèd devil
> Comes to himself again! we are undone.
> *Gasparo:* Strangle him in private.

It is the crowning suggestion which makes him cry out; the promise of forgetfulness is the "most fearful torment." [12]

There are several minor conventions fairly common in the drama. Marlowe's Duke of Guise (*Massacre at Paris*, sc. 18) is shocked by the manner of his death, and exclaims as he dies:

> O, that I have not power to stay my life,
> Or immortality to be reveng'd!
> To die by peasants, what a grief is this.

---

12. In Chapman's *Revenge for Honor* (IV, 2) the most effective curse is:

> May his black memory
> Perish even with his ashes!

And Hamlet's dying request is that his story be told to the world.

Death "by peasants" was considered a disgrace and an insult, whereas to die by a man of noble rank was complimentary and desirable. Marlowe's Guise is not alone in expressing this convention. Massinger's Domitian kills Paris himself (Paris had been caught with the Empress) and says (*Roman Actor*, IV, 2):

> let the honor
> I've done thee in thy death bring comfort to thee . . .
> . . . to confirm I loved thee, 'twas my study
> To make thy end more glorious, to distinguish
> My Paris from all others; and in that
> Have shown my pity.

But the convention is used in *2 Henry VI* with more emphasis than anywhere else, and the manner of its use shows how, even in the earlier drama, an attitude toward death might be indicative of character. The one thing that most offends proud Suffolk is that he is in danger of being killed by people of base rank.

> Obscure and lowly swain, King Henry's blood,
> The honorable blood of Lancaster
> Must not be shed by such a jaded groom,

he cries (IV, I). He cannot believe that such an event can occur;

> It is impossible that that I should die
> By such a lowly vassal as thyself,

and when it seems inevitable, his only consolation is that other great men have died in the same way, and that the infamy of such an outrage will make him remembered. The speech is characteristic of its time:

> Come, soldiers, show what cruelty ye can,
> That this my death may never be forgot.
> Great men oft die by vile bezonians,
> A Roman sworder and banditto slave
> Murder'd sweet Tully; Brutus' bastard hand
> Stabb'd Julius Caesar; savage islanders
> Pompey the Great; and Suffolk dies by pirates.[13]

The connection between death and the desire to preserve virginity was as common in Elizabethan drama as it has always been in literature. Whole plays were built around the belief that virginity accompanied by death is preferable to the loss of it accompanied by life. The Lucretia story (which Augustine had approved) [14] was used by Shake-

---

13. See also Heywood, *Rape of Lucrece* (v, 6):
> If I be killed amongst this hostile throng,
> The poorest snaky soldier well may claim
> As much renown in royal Sextus' death
> As Brutus, thou, or as thou Horatius. . . .
> Rob not yourselves of honor in my death!

Jonson, *Catiline*, IV, 2 (Catiline to Cicero):
> In vain dost thou conceive, ambitious orator,
> Hope of so brave a death as by this hand.

Fletcher, *Valentinian*, IV, 4 (Aëcius to the soldier who comes to kill him):
> Then so much the nobler, as thou wert a soldier,
> Shall my death be.

Massinger, *Duke of Milan*, v, 1 (another version of the convention):
> And but that
> I scorn a slave's base blood should rust that sword
> That from a prince expects a scarlet dye,
> Thou now wert dead.

14. *De Civitate Dei*, I, cap. xix. But though Augustine admired

speare in his poem on the subject, and by Heywood
in a very inferior play — *The Rape of Lucrece*. *The
Virgin Martyr* is constructed about virginity; it is the
central problem of *Measure for Measure*; and there
were many Elizabethan heroines who might have
remarked, like Marston's Sophonisba:

> All that I crave
> Is but chaste life, or an untainted grave.
> *(Sophonisba,* III, 1)

In *The Revenger's Tragedy* (I, 4) we are told that
Antonio's wife has killed herself because

> She, her honor forced,
> Deemed it a nobler dowry for her name
> To die with poison than to live with shame.

She was found lying dead with one prayer-book as
"the pillow to her cheek," and another held in her
right hand,

> With a leaf tucked up,
> Pointing to these words —
> *Melius virtute mori, quam per dedecus vivere,*

from which, no doubt, she took the hint. It was a
hint pretty frequently given.[15] For the situation of a
virgin and her would-be ravisher is admirable for

Lucretia's chastity, he rebuked her suicide: "Si adulterata cur
laudata; si pudica, cur occisa?"

15. A set speech in favor of virginity was one of the commonest
of Elizabethan conventions. R. S. Forsythe (*The Relations of
Shirley's Plays to the Elizabethan Drama,* New York, 1914, pp. 69–
70) cites twenty examples from Shirley and sixty-five from other
dramatists. A detailed study of these would be very interesting.

dramatic purposes, and the Elizabethans were much stronger believers in this particular convention than we. Shirley, always a master of the theatrical, if of nothing else, uses it to advantage in *The Traitor* (III, 3). The Duke approaches Amidea, and she shows him a poniard:

> *Duke:* Thou dar'st not kill me.
> *Amidea:* True, but I dare die.
> *Duke:* Be thy own murderer?
> *Amidea:* Rather than you should be my ravisher.

So Heywood's Lucrece (*Rape of Lucrece*, V, 1) exclaims, just before committing suicide:

> Let all the world learn of a Roman dame,
> To prize her life less than her honored fame.

> Better, than live unchaste, to lie in grave,

cries Ida, in Greene's *James IV* (II, 1); and the Duchess in Marston's *Malcontent* (V, 2) cries to her lover:

> O my dear'st Altofront! where'er thou breathe,
> Let my soul sink into the shades beneath,
> Before I stain thine honor! 'tis that thou has't,
> And long as I can die, I will live chaste.

In this matter the Elizabethans did not change the substance of the old convention at all, and virginity retained its place of honor unassailed — except by the most obvious of stage villains. It is worth noting that the moral sense appealed to in all dramatic representations of outraged virginity fits in exactly with St. Augustine's views on the subject. He had reluctantly lowered his ban on suicide in those cases where it was carried out in order to preserve chastity.[16] And where a woman, on the Elizabethan stage, commits suicide, she often does so to save her threatened virtue.

We shall return to the subject again; at the moment other matters demand our attention. It was considered essential for a man to have time to pray before he died, and when a murder was about to be committed, the intended victim urged his murderers to wait until he has prayed. "If you kill me now, I am damned; I have not been at confession this two years!" cries Cariola, the Duchess of Malfi's waiting maid (IV, 2), in a frantic effort to keep herself from being strangled. Mendoza in the *Malcontent* (V, 3) tries to stave off his death by the same method:

> O, lend me breath till I am fit to die!
> For peace with heaven, for your own souls' sake,
> Vouchsafe me life!

The Duke in *The Revenger's Tragedy* (II, 4), seeing murderers coming at him, cries:

> O, take me not in sleep!
> I have great sins; I must have days,
> Nay, months, dear son, with penitential heaves,
> To lift 'em out, and not to die unclear,
> O, thou wilt kill me both in Heaven and here.

---

16. See below, p. 159.

It is an old notion, and fits in, of course, with Bromyard's teaching about sudden death. It is also quite
in opposition to Montaigne's more classical idea of
wanting to die while planting cabbages. But Montaigne's idea (to my knowledge) does not directly
appear in the drama,[17] whereas its medieval opposite occurs not only as quoted above, but also
in Beaumont and Fletcher, Chapman, Tourneur,
Shirley, and Shakespeare.[18] In *Hamlet* Shakespeare

---

17. Unless we include the remark made by Flamineo (*White
Devil*, v, 6):

> Shoot, shoot:
> Of all deaths the violent death is best.

But Flamineo here knows he will not be shot; and his remark is
half-ironical, not to be taken too seriously.

18. *Philaster*, iv, 3:

> If your youth
> Have any way offended Heaven, let prayers
> Short and effectual reconcile you to it.

Chapman, *Tragedy of Byron*, iv, 2:

> Let me have the honor
> To die defending of my innocent self,
> And have some little space to pray to God.

Atheist's Tragedy, iv, 2:

> Perhaps he's praying. Then he's fit to die.
> We'll send him charitably to his grave.

The Traitor, v, 3: (the Duke, as he is about to be stabbed):

> Pity my poor soul;
> I have not prayed.

3 Henry VI, i, 3:

> *Rutland:* O! let me pray before I take my death!

Richard III, i, 4:

> *2nd Murderer:* Make peace with God, for you must die, my lord.

Measure for Measure, iv, 3 (Barnardine protests against execution):
"You rogue, I have been drinking all night; I am not fitted
for't."

Othello, v, 2:

reverses the convention; Hamlet will not kill his uncle while he is praying lest his soul should go to heaven rather than to hell, where it belongs. The use of a convention in this reverse fashion shows how powerful it is, and how useful it can be for dramatic purposes.

The belief that to die is to separate the soul and the body is very aged, perhaps as old as man himself. Ordinarily there is no image attached to it to give it life. But there is one exception to this rule which is striking. In the Middle Ages, as we have found already, the separation of body and soul at death was a terrible process — "the mast dred thing," said the author of *The Pricke of Conscience*, "in al this world." It was terrible, not only because the uprooting of the soul from the body was extraordinarily painful, but also because the dying man was attacked by the remembrance of his past sins and assailed by a host of devils waiting to snatch his soul.

Now Shakespeare, in the magnificent poetry with which he describes Clarence's dream (*Richard III*, I, 4), has the following lines:

Clarence: Lord, Lord! methought what pain it was to drown:

Othello: Have you pray'd to-night, Desdemona?
Desdemona: Ay, my lord.
Othello: If you bethink yourself of any crime
Unreconcil'd as yet to heaven and grace,
Solicit for it straight. . . .
No; heaven forfend! I would not kill thy soul.

> What dreadful noise of water in mine ears!
> What sights of ugly death within mine eyes! . . .
>
> Brackenbury: Awak'd you not with this sore agony?

And then Clarence gives the description of hell which I have quoted on page 119. If the reader will call that description to mind, he will remember that Clarence saw the shades of all those he had wronged rising up against him, and was environed with a "legion of foul fiends," who (in true medieval fashion) uttered "hideous cries." In other words, he underwent at death three of the four chief torments which the Middle Ages described as accompanying the moment of death (see above, pp. 10 ff.). He suffered "sore agony," he saw his past misdeeds, he was encompassed by devils. The only difference between Clarence's description and that of *The Pricke of Conscience* is that Clarence thinks himself in hell, whereas the dying man in *The Pricke of Conscience* is still on his deathbed when he sees the devils and his sins. But that is a minor point, and the change is what one would expect in a dramatic presentation; in every other respect the events described are virtually identical.[19] We cannot assume,

19. Deathbed devils occur at least twice in Elizabethan times outside the drama. Whetstone, *Rocke of Regard* (1576), ed. J. P. Collier (n.d.), p. 319, in a poem called "Frenos Complaint":

> My gracelesse deedes the hope of grace prevents.
>
> I see, I see, how fierie *fiendes* do *yell*,
>
> Before hie Jove my wicked soule to have.
>
> My secrete sinnes condemnes mee (wretch) to hell.

And Nashe, "Christs Teares," in *Works*, ed. R. B. McKerrow, of course, that Shakespeare knew *The Pricke of Conscience*, and he probably had not the slightest idea that he was even expressing an old convention, but the convention was there just the same, close to the surface, waiting to be transformed with additions and variations into poetry.

That the soldier's death was considered noble is another commonly expressed belief. We have seen it already in *Gorboduc*, and it occurs again in Chapman's *Tragedy of Byron* (v, 4):

> I will not die
> Like to a clergyman; but like the captain
> That pray'd on horseback, and with sword in hand,
> Threaten'd the sun, commanding it to stand.

Death, says the author of *Nero* (IV, 2),

> was not grim,
> But fair and lovely when he came in arms.[20]

This is a notion that has little to do with medieval teaching. But the next belief to be considered, that death is a punishment for sin, is a direct expression of the Christian doctrine which Calvinism had more

London, 1910, II, 115. Nashe is talking about atheists: "In the very houre of death shall appeare to them a God and a devill." Nashe then tells how a "grizly shaggy-bodied devill" appeared to "Atheisticall *Iulian*," and "hee recantingly cryed out, *Vicisti, Galilaee, vicisti*." At death, "those that never heard of God or the devill in theyr life before, at that instant of theyr transmutation shall gyve testimony of them."

20. See Middleton, *Changeling*, v, 2:
> I'll rather like a soldier die by th' sword,
> Than like a politician by thy poison.

than ever emphasized. In '*Tis Pity She's a Whore* we find the friar telling Giovanni that "death waits on thy lust" (I, I). Chapman's Tamyra (*Bussy D'Ambois*, III, I) remarks that since her surrender to her lust she is

> subject to the heartless fear
> Of every shadow,

whereas formerly, being virtuous, she "was secure against death and hell." But this old opinion does not occur frequently; it is not one that the drama made much use of.

There was another medieval idea which found a warmer welcome, the old notion that even Montaigne expressed: "The day of our death is the master-day, the day that is the judge of all the other days." There are plenty of characters in the drama who count on a good death to make up for the wickedness of their lives, just as most people had done in the Middle Ages. Sigismund in *2 Tamburlaine* (II, 3) addresses his God as follows:

> O just and dreadful punisher of sin,
> Let the dishonor of the pains I feel
> In this my mortal well-deserved wound
> End all my penance in my sudden death!
> And let this death, wherein to sin I die,
> Conceive a second life in endless mercy! —

a prayer which, even in its phrasing, has the true medieval ring. Aurelia in Marston's *Malcontent* (v, 3) makes a remark of a similar kind:

> Death gives eternity a glorious breath:
> O, to die honor'd, who would fear to die?

But this is not entirely in the medieval spirit; the desire for fame was becoming a part of even the most orthodox Christian ideas.   In Fletcher's *Bonduca*, too, we have the notion given a non-Christian twist. Bonduca's first daughter commits suicide (IV, 4), saying:

> Live as you have done, well . . . ,
> So shall ye learn the noblest part, to die.

When Gaunt dies (*Richard II*, II, 1) he expresses the old belief in combination with another: the belief that a man's last words are of particular importance:

> O! but they say the tongues of dying men
> Enforce attention like deep harmony . . .
> More are men's ends mark'd than their lives before.

Shakespeare uses the convention again, in a well-known passage (*Macbeth*, I, 4). Malcolm describes the death of the rebellious earl of Cawdor:

> Very frankly he confess'd his treasons,
> Implor'd your highness' pardon and set forth
> A deep repentance.   Nothing in his life
> Became him like the leaving it; he died
> As one that had been studied in his death
> To throw away the dearest thing he ow'd
> As 'twere a careless trifle.

Here we are meant to be moved (though perhaps only slightly) by Cawdor's death; and in order that such emotion be produced, we must have in our minds the belief that a good death is admirable. Poet and audience rely on the convention, and its presence in the minds of both makes the communication of emotion from one to the other possible.

Another stock idea that the Middle Ages passed on to the Elizabethan drama was that a king, no matter how much land he had when he was alive, would only have the dominion of his grave when he was dead.

> Lo! now my glory smear'd in dust and blood . . .
> and of all my lands
> Is nothing left me but my body's length.
> Why, what is pomp, rule, reign, but earth and dust?
> And, live we how we can, yet die we must,

says Warwick (*3 Henry VI*, v, 2). And not only does Warwick make the old remark; he also follows it up with the old moral, expressed in language as stale as itself. Far more vivid is the passage in *Richard II* (III, 2). King Richard is speaking:

> Our lands, our lives, and all are Bolingbroke's,
> And nothing can we call our own but death,
> And that small model of the barren earth
> Which serves as paste and cover to our bones,

and again (III, 3):

> I'll give . . .
> . . . my large kingdom for a little grave,
> A little little grave, an obscure grave.[21]

---

21. See *1 Henry IV* (v, 4): (Prince Henry addressing Hotspur's body):

There are several other notions of less interest which we may pass over more hurriedly. Death, for example, involves the loss of all worldly things, the end of all worldly activities. The gaoler in *Cymbeline* (v, 4) refers light-heartedly to the fact: "A heavy reckoning for you, sir; but the comfort is, you shall be called to no more payments, fear no more tavern-bills." Other dramatic characters refer to the same obvious notion in a more serious way. Nero in the play which goes by his name (v, 3) is tormented by the thought of leaving the world:

> Alas, how sharp and terrible is death!
> Oh, must I die, must now my senses close;
> For ever die, and ne'er return again,
> Never more see the sun, nor heaven, nor earth?

And we have it again, in that vein of pathos which is as typical of the decaying Elizabethan drama as it is of the decaying Greek:

Thierry: Suppose it death!
Ordella: I do.
Thierry: And endless parting
    With all we can call ours, with all our sweetness,

> Ill-weav'd ambition, how much art thou shrunk!
> When that this body did contain a spirit,
> A kingdom for it was too small a bound;
> But now, two paces of the vilest earth
> Is room enough;

and *Julius Caesar* (iii, 1):

> O mighty Caesar! dost thou lie so low?
> Are all thy conquests, glories, triumphs, spoils,
> Shrunk to this little measure?

> With youth, strength, pleasure, people, time, nay,
>   reason?
> For in the silent grave, no conversation,
> No joyful tread of friends, no voice of lovers,
> No careful father's counsel; nothing's heard
> Nor nothing is, but all oblivion,
> Dust and an endless darkness: and dare you, woman,
> Desire this place?
>   (Fletcher, *Thierry and Theodoret*, IV, 1)

This melancholy music, which at its best is true pathos, and at its worst is sentimentality, is common in Fletcher. Like Euripides after Sophocles, the emotion he plays upon is pity; the terror of great tragedy has passed away, the iron gone out of its blood.

This is clearly to be seen in a favorite device of Fletcher's by which he reverses the usual feeling about death, and instead of considering it something horrible, turns it into something pretty and agreeable.

> Oh, death, thou art more than beauty, and thy pleasure
> Beyond posterity!

exclaims Aëcius in *Valentinian* (IV, 4).

> Do it, worthy sister;
> 'Tis nothing; 'tis a pleasure,

urges one of Bonduca's daughters (*Bonduca*, IV, 4), when she is trying to make her sister commit suicide. But the most striking use of this attitude is in the scene from *Thierry and Theodoret* which I have just quoted, for Thierry's attempt to make death as dis-

agreeable as possible to Odella elicits only the following reply:

> 'Tis of all sleeps the sweetest:
> Children begin it to us, strong men seek it,
> And kings from height of all their painted glories
> Fall like spent exhalations to this centre:
> And those are fools that fear it, or imagine
> A few unhandsome pleasures or life's profits
> Can recompense this place.

This is an easy way to produce admiring tears in
an audience, and it was probably more effective in
Elizabethan times than it would be today; the
Elizabethans were more intimate than we are with
the conviction that only the best and purest characters are anxious to die. Fletcher was consciously
playing on the emotion which would be automatically stirred up by a reference to this Christian belief, and the device was clearly successful or he
would not have used it so often.

Such facile emotionalism is frequent in Fletcher's
death-bed scenes, and a dying character, full of
gentle resignation, often pathetically asks to be remembered after he has gone. A speech like that of
Aëcius (*Valentinian*, IV, 4) is positively viscid with
sentiment:

> When I am dead, speak honorably of me,
> That is, preserve my memory from dying;
> Then, if you needs must weep your ruined master,
> A tear or two will seem well. This I charge ye
> (Because ye say you yet love old Aëcius,)

> See my poor body burnt, and some to sing
> About my pile, and what I have done and suffered,
> If Caesar kill not that too: at your banquets,
> When I am gone, if any chance to number
> The times that have been sad and dangerous,
> Say how I fell, and 'tis sufficient.[22]

Fletcher, as has been frequently pointed out, is thoroughly romantic, and in no way does his romanticism show more clearly than in his treatment of death. His Aspatia (*Maid's Tragedy*, I, I) has Fletcher's own habits:

> when the rest
> Of our young ladies, in their wanton blood,
> Tell mirthful tales in course, that fill the room
> With laughter, she will, with so sad a look,
> Bring forth a story of the silent death
> Of some forsaken virgin, which her grief
> Will put in such a phrase that, ere she end,
> She'll send them weeping one by one away.

And Aspatia a little later illustrates this practice by making a pathetic speech about herself, which was intended to make the audience weep — though not, perhaps, to send them away:

> Ladies, farewell. As soon as I am dead,
> Come all and watch one night about my hearse;
> Bring each a mournful story and a tear,

---

22. See *Philaster*, III, I:
> Farewell for evermore!
> If you shall hear that sorrow struck me dead,
> And after find me loyal, let there be
> A tear shed from you in my memory,
> And I shall rest at peace.

> To offer at it when I go to earth;
> With flattering ivy clasp my coffin round;
> Write on my brow my fortune; let my bier
> Be borne by virgins, that shall sing by course
> The truth of maids and perjuries of men.
>
> (II, I)

A true tragic heroine would not think it necessary to arrange for her funeral like this; her character and situation, as with Sophocles and Shakespeare, would make her tragic, not these pathetic accidents. Nor would it be any but a romantic character who would say, as Aspatia does:

> So with my prayers I leave you, and must try
> Some yet *unpractised* way to grieve and die.[23]

But these notions — that with death the world is lost, and that a dying character craves post-mortem attention — are chiefly worth notice as traps for writers who lack emotional intensity.

23. Italics mine. The "when I am dead and gone" motive appears also in *Bonduca*, v, 5:
> Pray for me;
> And, noble uncle, when my bones are ashes,
> Think of your little nephew!

This sentiment is, of course, used in the earlier plays too, but not in this manner. In *2 Henry VI*, II, 3, Gloucester says:
> Farewell, good king! when I am dead and gone,
> May honorable peace attend thy throne;

which is a much nobler wish than those expressed by Beaumont and Fletcher's characters. Shakespeare uses it too, briefly, in *Hamlet*, v, 2:
> Absent thee from felicity awhile,
> And in this harsh world draw thy breath in pain,
> To tell my story.

More interesting is the repetition of the medieval idea of the necessity and advantages of thinking about death. We find it vividly expressed in *The Old Law*, by Middleton, Massinger, and Rowley (v, 1):

> My sins and I [says Lysander]
> Have been but newly parted; much ado
> I had to get them leave me, or be taught
> That difficult lesson, how to learn to die.
> I never thought there had been such an art,
> And 'tis the only discipline we are born for:
> All studies else are but as circular lines,
> And death the centre where they must all meet.

Nothing could be more medieval than that; except for the language, it might have been written in the fourteenth century. Nor is this the only occasion on which we find this familiar notion: it is also implied in the description Shakespeare gives us of Barnardine (*Measure for Measure*, IV, 2):

Provost: A man that apprehends death no more dreadfully but as a drunken sleep; careless, reckless, and fearless of what's past, present or to come; insensible of mortality, and desperately mortal.
Duke: He wants advice.

And we know what the advice would have been, for the Duke has already given it to Claudio (III, 1; above, p. 115): "Be absolute for death," he urges, and consider that life is nothing, "a thing that none but fools would keep."

A natural desire connected with death, which the characters of Elizabethan drama occasionally expressed, was to have, as the Duchess of Malfi phrased it (IV, 2), "some two days' conference with the dead." Flamineo in *The White Devil* (v, 4) questions the ghost of Brachiano, who stalks past him:

> In what place art thou? in yon starry gallery?
> Or in the cursèd dungeon? — No? not speak?
> Pray, sir, resolve me, what religion's best
> For a man to die in? or is it in your knowledge
> To answer me how long I have to live?

But the ghost is silent, and Flamineo's question, like the wish of the Duchess, remains unanswered. Shirley uses this desire ironically. Lorenzo, in *The Traitor* (IV, 2), says to Sciarrha:

> Go practice immortality,
> And tell us, when you can get leave to visit
> This world again, what fine things you enjoy
> In hell.

That death destroys death was a common conceit of the time. Shakespeare uses it in the most conventionally religious of his sonnets (CXLVI): addressing his soul, he urges it to buy "terms divine" rather than to spend its time on earthly "dross";

> So shalt thou feed on Death, that feeds on men,
> And Death once dead, there's no more dying then.

And in *Richard II* (III, 2) Carlisle remarks:

> And fight and die is death destroying death.[24]

---

24. Donne ends his most famous sonnet:
  One short sleepe past, wee wake eternally,
  And death shall be no more; death, thou shalt die.
But to my knowledge this idea is not fully developed till nearly

3

It may be said that the drama uses nearly all the ideas about death that had been passed on to it from the past. Since the dramatists of Elizabeth's time were deliberately playing upon the emotions of their audiences, they employed, in the various ways we have mentioned, practically every moral notion the Middle Ages had given them, and a good many which they borrowed from the classics.

It has doubtless been noticed that the triteness of these notions is extreme. Most of them would occur to the mind of anyone who considers, however briefly, the effect of death. But their very triteness gives them interest. They are the common property, not only of the Elizabethans, but of ourselves. The chief difference between the Elizabethans and ourselves is that we, perhaps ashamed of their flatness, rarely express them in poetry. But they are still expressed in all the most broadly popular forms of art, for they carry with them, rubbed smooth by constant use though they are, considerable emotional power; they are continually being re-experienced. A platitude comes to life for the individual when he suddenly realizes its truth as applied to a

---

two hundred years after Shakespeare's time. The American poet, Philip Freneau, has a long and striking poem called "The House of Night," in which the death of Death is described.

particular instance; and in this realization, though his enthusiasm may afterwards be chilled by noticing that it *is* a platitude, he experiences all the excitement of a discovery.

It is this fact which makes the platitude so successful in the drama. The action of a play supplies the particular instance which revivifies it, and brings it home to the audience (a fact which, incidentally, is the basis of the moralist's support of the theatre). In other words, these common notions, flat and meaningless as they appear when stated apart from their application, come to life on the stage. Not always, of course; for one must remember that before they come to life in the audience, they must be experienced and "discovered" by the dramatist. It is doubtful if Marston was much moved when he made his heroine remark,

> All that I crave
> Is but chaste life, or an untainted grave.

But the case is different with Shakespeare's Isabella; there emotion *has* infused the old tradition, and it enjoys a little renaissance of its own.

The same phenomenon, that is, took place in connection with thoughts and ideas as with words and phrases. There existed a collection of opinions, of ancient beliefs and traditions, which the individual drew upon almost subconsciously whenever he pleased, and used as his situation demanded. These became emotional or not just as they affected the dramatist, and as they affected the dramatist (owing to the peculiarities of rhythm as a means of communication) they, perhaps to a less degree, affected the audience as well. Frequently these ideas, like the words and phrases, became transformed, and were turned slightly from their previous positions to reflect the new situation which they illustrated. Indeed the quality of a poet's mind may best be judged by observing how much he *does* change these hereditary ideas, just as his poetic ability is largely determined by the way he changes his hereditary vocabulary.

In order to see more clearly how this applies, it will be appropriate to end this chapter with a full discussion of one particular problem which underwent striking changes at the hands of the Elizabethan dramatists — the problem of suicide.

That suicide was violently disapproved of by the medieval Church is well known.[25] Though nothing is said about it in the New Testament, the Jewish historian Josephus, who exercised much influence on early Christian writers, maintained that suicide was not only a crime against nature, but also against God, and that those who killed themselves were "received by the darkest place in Hades." [26] St.

25. For a full discussion of the history of suicide, see A Bayet, *Le Suicide et la Morale*, Paris, 1922. For further references H. Rost, *Bibliographie des Selbstmords*, Augsburg, 1927, may be consulted.

26. *Bel. Jud.*, III, VIII, 5, Whiston's trans.

Augustine [27] opposed suicide on the grounds that it precluded the possibility of repentance, and that as a form of homicide it violated the sixth commandment. But Augustine was forced to allow that it was respectable in some cases, since several persons who had committed suicide to preserve their virginity were recognized as martyrs. The church council of Bragues in 563, however, and that of Auxerre in 578, forbade masses to be said for suicides.

"Who is more capable of mortal sin," said Pope Nicholas I, "than the fool, who, imitating Judas, follows the teaching of the devil and kills himself?" [28] Abelard [29] decided against suicide. St. Thomas Aquinas produced three reasons against it: it violated charity and self-love; it offended both human and divine laws of citizenship; and it usurped the rights of God.[30] And we have only to remember the thirteenth canto of the *Inferno* to know what Dante thought about the subject.

Secular law reflected the opinion of the Church. In early France jurisdiction over suicides was left to

27. *De Civ. Dei*, I, caps. XVII ff.

28. *Responsa ad Consulta Bulgarorum*, art. XCVIII, ap. Labb, V, IX, p. 1565. I take this, as well as several other references, from F. Bourquelot, "Recherches sur les opinions et la legislation en matière de mort volontaire, pendant le moyen age," in *Bibliothèque de l'École des Chartes*, 1st series, III (1841–1842), 539 ff.; IV (1842–1843), 242 ff.; an excellent article to which I am much indebted on this matter.

29. *Sic et Non*, cap. CLIV.

30. *Summa Theologica*, 2, 2a, q. LXIV, a. 5; and 2, 2a, q. LIX, a. 3.

the secular authorities; and they even went so far as to bring proceedings against the corpse; if it was found guilty, it was hanged, quartered, and thrown into the public sewer, while the suicide's property was confiscated in favor of his feudal lord or the King. Even the attempt at suicide was regarded as criminal. However, suicide was excused when it was committed in a moment of mental alienation or as a result of intense sorrow; [31] and we are told by the thirteenth-century jurist, Philippe de Beau-manoir, that if it is uncertain whether a man's death is intentional or accidental, it is better not to forfeit the goods or maltreat the corpse.[32]

But in spite of these palliating reservations, suicide was unquestionably condemned. It was condemned by the Church and made terrible by law (the corpse of a suicide was maltreated in order to frighten others from following such an example), and one would therefore imagine that the number of suicides in the Middle Ages was smaller than in other periods of history. This, however, is a difficult question to determine. Suicides, when they occurred in monasteries, were naturally hushed up, and no record of them was preserved. And it is plain

31. I take this information from C. L. von Bar, *A History of Continental Criminal Law*, trans. T. S. Bell, Boston, 1916, p. 187, and the references there given.

32. *Les Coutumes de Beauvoisis*, ed. Salmon, Paris, 1900, ii, 485, sec. 1952: "Car l'en ne doit pas croire que nus se mete a mort a escient s'il n'est prouvé clerement ou par apertes presompcions."

that plenty of suicides did occur under Christianity. There had been, in the fourth century, a Christian sect known as the Circumcelliones, the members of which sometimes leaped from high cliffs and dashed themselves to pieces on the rocks below; the Albigensian heretics, eight centuries later, indulged in a practice, which they called Endura, of accelerating death, in the case of dangerous illness, by fasting and sometimes by bleeding.[33] Many medieval Jews committed suicide to escape from the hell life was made for them. The ascetic practices of the saints probably hastened death in many cases, and the monastic vice of acedia undoubtedly caused a certain number of monks to do away with themselves. Occasionally, too, a kind of mass-suicide occurred. In 1095, a multitude died by their own hands in France to avoid torture; at a later date, five hundred killed themselves at York, and the Black Death apparently caused a number of people to destroy themselves during the period of its most violent raging.[34] Suicide, as a fact, was by no means uncommon during the Middle Ages, though all authoritative teaching, and all the emphasis of the Church, was strongly against it.[35]

33. Lecky, *European Morals*, New York, 1929, II, 49.
34. *Ibid.*, II, 51.
35. The Reformation in no way changed the medieval attitude to the subject. Burckhardt, in his *Civilization of the Renaissance in Italy*, Eng. tr., London, 1898, p. 277, refers to Pierio Valeriano's *De Infelicitate Literatorum* (written 1527) for mention of suicide in sixteenth-century Italy.

In the fashionable literature of the Middle Ages, however, suicide was treated in a different manner. For in spite of the fact that anyone who committed suicide was, according to the priests, certain to go to hell, in the medieval romances the act itself and expressions of a desire to indulge in it were frequent. The convention of love, which demanded that suicide be immediately considered at any hint of disappointment, had its own standards which practically never touched the standards of the Church; literature and life were kept rigorously apart.[36]

This literary convention naturally lasted into the sixteenth century; for example, Whetstone, in his *Rocke of Regard*, tells us the old-fashioned story of Rinaldo and Giletta in which the hero, when he thinks his lady unfaithful to him, immediately tries to drown himself in the river Po. But in spite of such narratives (and there are plenty of them),[37] the sixteenth century, in this matter as in so many others, gradually broke down the partitions which the Middle Ages had set up between life and story-telling, and when suicide occurred in literature more thought was given it; it was related to other than purely literary conventions.[38]

36. For a discussion of this see Bourquelot, *art. cit.*

37. See Bandello, *Novelle*, Lucca, 1554, I, nos. 8, 20, 43, 50.

38. William Painter, *Palace of Pleasure* (1566; ed. J. Jacobs, London, 1890, tom. II, nov. 9), tells of "A straunge and marvellous use, which in old time was observed in Hidrusa, where it was lawfull, with the licence of a magistrate ordayned for that purpose, for every man, and woman that list, to kill them selves." An

The most striking example of this is the well-known passage in the first book of *The Faerie Queene* (canto IX, 33 ff.), where Spenser tells how Despair urges the Red Cross Knight to kill himself. The tone which the subject demands fits Spenser's melody well, and the passage is among the most effective he ever wrote. "Why should I not help men on their way to death?" asks Despair; in death there is rest and happy ease, and the life of man, perplexed by a thousand ills, oppressed by innumerable sins, were better brought quickly to an end:

> what then must needs be donne,
> Is it not better to doe willinglie,
> Then linger, till the glasse be all out ronne?
> Death is the end of woes: die soone, O faeries sonne.
>
> (st. 47)

The Knight's resistance is overcome; he seizes a knife, and is on the point of stabbing himself when Una rushes forward to rescue him. For he had to be

---

example is given, and a trite moral applied. *The Mirror for Magistrates* includes several suicide stories: "How Queene Cordila in dispaire slew her selfe, B.C. 800," for example (ed. J. Haslewood, London, 1815, I, 123). The Emperor Nero commits suicide (I, 300, st. 16), saying:

> My life was filthy, vile for to beholde,
> My death more vile shall bee, more filthy I departe:
> With that I fell on sword, which ran me through the harte.

Sackville in his "Induction" (st. 74) is less moral. Among the old maids in hell, he sees

> the guiltles slayne, and lovers dead,
> That slew them selves when nothing els avayld

— a description which, if it carries with it any judgment at all, is tolerant enough, and fits in well with the medieval convention of love.

saved: if he had committed suicide, he would have been proved a coward; and even his yielding as he did to the old man's arguments makes it later necessary for him to spend a long time in purification.[39]

Such was the usual feeling on the matter, and the rather shallow mind of Spenser gives a clear picture of it. Wiser men were less positive. Montaigne writes about suicide at some length in his *Essays* (bk. II, 3 and 13), but, following his custom when discussing ideas, does not commit himself. He gives all the arguments for suicide, then all the arguments against it, and proceeds to quote a number of anecdotes instead of coming to a decision. Yet if we read between the lines, we can see that, though Montaigne's character would have prevented him from ever committing suicide himself, he considers it occasionally permissible. "Intolerable pain and the fear of a worse death appear to me to be the most excusable inducements," he says, and there are many

---

39. A few years after this (1596), Spenser's ideas were repeated by Anthony Copley in *A Fig For Fortune* (ed. Spenser Society [1883]). Dressed in black and considerably depressed, the poet met the ghost of Cato, who

rear'd his mongrel-lumpe up towards me,
Fainting and falling in his Deaths-disgrace,

and then proceeded to give every possible argument for suicide. Death is a welcome release, and since "there is no hell like to declined glorie" (a typical Renaissance observation), the best thing to do is to get out of life as soon as possible. Copley was convinced, and decided to kill himself. But before he could do so Cato's ghost suddenly disappeared, leaving a horrible smell of sulphur behind, and Copley ends by thanking God that he had been saved in time.

men who have committed suicide, especially Cato, whom he thoroughly admires.[40]

This unresolved attitude seems to have been fairly widespread. "Les Romains pouvaient faire cela," says Monluc; "les chrétiens, non." [41] Lipsius, in his *Manuductio ad Stoicam Philosophiam*, explains the Stoic idea of suicide sympathetically, but ends by contradicting it, on account of "the laws of our religion." [42] And Montaigne's disciple, Charron, though he urges his reader to despise death, urges him with equal force not to commit suicide; it is "plus lâcheté, que courage; c'est, de plus, mal raisonner. . . . Il fallait donc attendre." [43]

Thus, about the year 1600, there were three ways of thinking of suicide: it was admired in the heroes of antiquity; it was resorted to by virtuous women and the chief characters in a love story; it was heartily condemned by the prevailing religion.

But shortly after this date a new opinion, stepping tentatively, hesitatingly, looking over its shoulder with frightened glances, finally made its appearance. About 1608 John Donne wrote a work called *Bia-*

40. An interesting essay could be written on the various attitudes to Cato in the Middle Ages and the Renaissance. Copley and Montaigne represent the two extremes: the vulgar and the aristocratic; the ignorant and the well-read. The difference of opinion seems to be largely a matter of education and reading.

41. *Memoires*, Paris, 1865, I, 275; quoted in Bayet, *Le Suicide et la Morale*, Paris, 1922, p. 538.

42. Bayet, *op. cit.*, p. 531.

43. *De la Sagesse*, Paris, 1827, II, 235.

thanatos: A Declaration of that Paradoxe, or Thesis, that selfe-homicide is not so naturally sinne, that it may never be otherwise. Even the title is very cautious; so were Donne's directions about what should be done with the manuscript of the work itself: it was neither to be printed nor burnt.[44] It was, however, printed in 1646 by Donne's son, who evidently shared his father's views, for he remarked in his dedicatory letter that "although this Booke appeare under the notion of a Paradox, yet, I desire your Lordship, to looke upon this Doctrine, as a firme and established truth."

The book is negligible as literature, subtle and involved as philosophy, overweighted as scholarship, and profoundly interesting for our purpose. For it is the first serious attempt I am aware of, after Christianity,[45] to establish suicide as a praiseworthy act.

44. Cf. Donne's letter to Sir Robert Carre sent with a MS. copy of *Biathanatos* in 1619 (*Letters to Severall Persons of Honor*, ed. C. E. Merrill, Jr., New York, 1910, p. 19): "It was written by me many years since; and because it is upon a misinterpretable subject, I have always gone so near suppressing it, as that it is onely not burnt: no hand hath passed upon it to copy it, nor many eyes to read it: onely to some particular friends in both Universities, then when I writ it, I did communicate it: And I remember, I had this answer, That certainly, there was a false thread in it, but not easily found: Keep it, I pray, with the same jealousie; let any that your discretion admits to the sight of it, know the date of it; and that it is a Book written by *Jack Donne* and not by Dr. *Donne*: Reserve it for me, if I live, and if I die, I only forbid it the Presse, and the Fire: publish it not, but yet burn it not; and between those, do what you will with it."

45. Sir Thomas More, to be sure, had spoken favorably of

We may find Augustine allowing suicide as an alternative to violation, and medieval law and medieval romance condoning it when committed under the influence of headstrong passion; we may find Montaigne speaking of it at least without disapprobation; but hitherto we have not discovered anyone who seriously and laboriously set out to disprove orthodox teaching on the subject. No wonder that Donne's performance is timorous and wavering. His introduction is apologetic, and his treatment so overfreighted with quotations and examples that one imagines him to have made it ponderous on purpose, so that none but the scholars for whom he claimed he was writing would care to read it.[46]

I have not space to give more than a very brief outline of the book; nor would it be especially

---

suicide in his *Utopia*, but it is not at all clear how seriously he meant the work to be taken, and his reference to the matter is in a different spirit from Donne's. Mr. T. E. Terrill (*Spanish Influence on John Donne*, Harvard MS. dissertation, 1928, pp. 98 ff.) has suggested that the source of *Biathanatos* is the *De Homicidio* of Francisco de Vitoria (1486?–1546). But Francisco's treatise is only 25 12mo. pages long (not 56, as Mr. Terrill says), and merely a few paragraphs are about suicide. How different the thought is from Donne's may be shown by quoting one sentence (cap. 36): "Unde non solum qui se interficiunt, sed qui sine alio titulo ponunt vitam in magno periculo propter gloriam humanam, graviter delinquunt."

46. He makes the work scholarly, he tells us in his introduction (1646 ed., p. 23), "because scholastique and artificiall men use this way of instructing; and I made account that I was to deale with such, because I presume that naturall men are at least enough inclinable of themselves to this doctrine," e.g. suicide — a significant commentary.

profitable to do so, for its chief interest for us is not so much in a detailed account of what it says as in the fact that it was written at all. It is divided into three parts. In the first Donne tries to show that suicide is not against the law of Nature: suicide has been common at all times, there is nothing against it in the Scriptures, and the early Church practically encouraged it by its emphasis on martyrdom, which is suicide at one remove: "This desire of Martyrdome . . . swallowed up all the other inducements [to death], which, before Christianity contracted them, tickled and inflamed mankinde" (I, dist. III, sec. 6).

The second book shows that suicide is not contrary to the law of reason: Roman law has nothing against it, canon law does not definitely call it a sin, and English law (which confiscated the goods of the suicide) was only necessary because suicide was formerly prevalent owing to the poor condition of slaves and laborers. Then Donne takes up various opinions against it and refutes them; he speaks of practices, fasting and the like, which are almost suicide and yet are allowed by ecclesiastical authority.

The third book tries to prove that suicide does not violate the law of God. Christ's death was heroic, yet did he not bring it on himself? Besides, as we know, there is nothing against suicide in the Scriptures. Nevertheless a man should not commit suicide thoughtlessly. "Wee say . . . that this may be

done onely, when the honor of God may bee pro-
moved by that way, and no other " (III, dist. v, sec.
4). And the conclusion, which is worth quoting at
some length, is as follows:

> So I may say of this case, that in punishment of *Adams* sinne,
> God cast upon us an infectious death, and since hath sent us a
> worse plague of men, which accompanie it with so much horror
> and affrightment, that it can scarce be made wholsome and
> agreeable to us. . . . But though I thought it therefore need-
> full, to oppose this defensative, as well to re-encourage men to
> a just contempt of this life, and to restore them to their nature,
> which is a desire of supreame happines in the next life by the
> losse of this, as also to rectify, and wash again their fame, who
> religiously assuring themselves that in some cases, when wee
> were destitute of other meanes, we might be to our selves the
> stewards of Gods benefits, and the Ministers of his mercifull
> Justice. . . . For, that is certainly true of this, which Cassianus
> saith of a ly, [that it hath the nature of Ellebore, wholsome in
> desperate diseases, but otherwise poyson].

The book is not, then, so radical after all, nor
would it be more than a shallow expectation that
would count on its being so. Donne was by no means
an ethical revolutionary, and it is natural that in
considering suicide as sometimes defensible he
should not only wrap his opinions in the wool of
scholarship, but, when coming to the end of them,
he should make them seem as tame as possible by
fitting them into conventional ideas; he was hardly
original when he pointed to the next world as a better
place than this one.

We must not, however, underestimate the importance of *Biathanatos*. In spite of its timid expression and its tentative presentation, it does, after all, represent the first serious treatment of suicide as worthy of commendation; and to come across it after so many senseless repetitions of the older notions is, in a way, a relief. It shows, as so much of our study has shown, how the Elizabethans were questioning the conceptions they had inherited from their ancestors.

We find suicides everywhere in Elizabethan drama. In the *Spanish Tragedy*, Isabella and Hieronimo commit suicide, the latter without any reflections on his act, the former with a knowledge, apparently, that she is doing something she will be punished for:

> So shall my womb be cursed for his [Horatio's] sake.
>
> (IV, 2)

Hieronimo, too, has had thoughts of doing away with himself before he finally brings the play to an end by putting a knife through his heart. As he enters with a poniard in one hand and a rope in the other, he says:

> . . . Soft and fair, not so:
> For if I hang or kill myself, let's know
> Who will revenge Horatio's murder then?
>
> (III, 12)

The subject is here treated from two angles. It is either mentioned in connection with the old con-

demnation or is considered in relation to a dramatic necessity. When Isabella kills herself, she has
Christianity vaguely in her mind; when Hieronimo
thinks of suicide, he takes into account only revenge.

This double treatment is frequently found in the
Elizabethan plays. Romeo and Juliet destroy them-
selves because of the intensity of their love and the
unbearableness of its frustration; Antony and
Cleopatra do the same thing; Antonio's wife in *The
Revenger's Tragedy* (I, 4) and Heywood's Lucrece
commit suicide when their honor has been lost.
Evadne and Amintor kill themselves in the *Maid's
Tragedy* (v, 4), the one because of despairing pas-
sion, the other so that he may join his mistress.
"Here's to be with thee, love!" cries Amintor, and
stabs himself. Levidulcia, in *The Atheist's Tragedy*
(IV, 5), has a more moral purpose. With her lover
and her husband lying dead before her, she says:

> To make the example move more forceably
> To virtue, thus I seal it with a death
> As full of horror as my life of sin.

And, since she has a dagger in her hand, it is easy to
imagine what she does. But her remarks as she does
it, like Isabella's, are entirely of the Middle Ages.

In Fletcher's *Valentinian* (IV, 4) we have a curious
mingling of two ideas. Aëcius, giving some last advice to his friends before his execution, says:

> Yet fear a wilful death; the just gods hate it —

an observation medieval enough. But a little later, when his servant Pontius kills himself, Aëcius takes quite another attitude:

> Thou has deceived me, Pontius, and I thank thee:
> By all my hopes in Heaven, thou art a Roman! . . .
>   Thou hast fashioned death
> In such an excellent and beauteous manner,
> I wonder men can live.

Aëcius, indeed, becomes enthusiastic on the subject:

> Is there an hour of goodness beyond this?
> Or any man would out-live such a dying? . . .
> Oh, death, thou art more than beauty, and thy pleasure
> Beyond posterity!

And he falls on his sword, still rhapsodical. It is a curious juxtaposition; but we have already seen enough of the way in which clashing ideas are jumbled in the drama not to be surprised at it.

It is hardly necessary to give further examples. Hamlet's two soliloquies on the subject are well known, and they would lose much of their point if we, like the Elizabethan audience, did not feel grave doubts as to the advisability of suicide — doubts which are as much the result of the "humana conditio" as of the Middle Ages.[47]

Thus the drama treats suicide in the same three

---

47. Some further references to suicide are: *White Devil*, v, 6 (Vittoria to Flamineo, thinking him about to kill himself):
> Are you grown an atheist? will you turn your body,
> Which is the goodly palace of the soul,
> To the soul's slaughter-house?

ways the Renaissance as a whole had treated it. It
is notable that in this matter, as in their treatment
of the other world, the dramatists seem to have been
fairly careful about anachronisms: "Les Romains

There is much more in the same strain, some of it taken verbatim
from Montaigne, whose remarks, interestingly enough, are used
to fit into the traditional beliefs about the outrageousness of suicide
— a purpose he hardly intended them for.

Fletcher, *Bonduca*, IV, 3 and 4. Poenius, a defeated general, kills
himself; so do Bonduca and her daughters:

> "Do it, worthy sister;
>   'Tis nothing; 'tis a pleasure."

And this being a Roman play, such actions are commended.

Fletcher, *Thierry and Theodoret*, IV, 1. This being a "Christian"
play, the opposite opinion is taken. Ordella is discouraged from
suicide by Martellus:

> Where or how
> Got you these bloody thoughts? what devil durst
> Look on that angel-face and tempt? do you know
> What 'tis to die thus? how you strike the stars
> And all good things above? do you feel
> What follows a self-blood? whither you venture,
> And to what punishment?

Nero, IV, 6: Seneca's suicide described commendingly.

Julius Caesar, V, 1: Brutus speaks, and infuses into a Roman atmosphere the Christian notion:

> Even by the rule of that philosophy
> By which I did blame Cato for the death
> Which he did give himself; I know not how,
> But I do find it cowardly and vile,
> For fear of what might fall, so to prevent
> The time of life.

Yet Brutus does kill himself (V, 5):

> Our enemies have beat us to the pit:
> It is more worthy to leap in ourselves,
> Than tarry till they push us.

Othello, V, 2: Othello, made desperate by events, kills himself —
without, fortunately, any reflections of a moral kind which would
destroy the situation.

pouvaient faire cela; les chrétiens, non." Suicide
was, indeed, one of the best ways of giving a Roman
atmosphere to a play. Shakespeare shows clearly
how the Elizabethans, unlike the people of the Middle Ages, realized the difference between Roman
customs and their own when he makes Horatio say,
expressing a desire for suicide:

> I am more an antique Roman than a Dane.

But there are two important plays which completely escape these limitations and which treat
suicide in an entirely original fashion. They are
Chapman's *Caesar and Pompey* and the same author's *Revenge of Bussy D'Ambois.* They were both,
apparently, written about the same time (1610–13),[48]

King Lear, IV, 6: Gloucester repents of his attempt to kill himself:
> You ever-gentle gods, take my breath from me:
> Let not my worser spirit tempt me again
> To die before you please!

and again (Edgar to Gloucester, V, 2):
> What! in ill thoughts again?   Men must endure
> Their going hence, even as their coming hither:
> Ripeness is all.   Come on.
> *Glou:* And that's true too.

Massinger, *Maid of Honor*, II, 4: Ferdinand is hard pressed by a
siege:
> How willingly, like Cato,
> Could I tear out my bowels, rather than
> Look on the conqueror's insulting face;
> But that religion, and the horrid dream
> To be suffered in the other world, denies it!

Webster, *Appius and Virginia*, IV, 2: Virginius offers to kill himself,
since the act of suicide is nothing to the hand that killed his daughter.

48. See *The Tragedies of George Chapman*, ed. T. M. Parrott,
London, 1910, p. 655.

and since it has never been certainly determined which preceded the other, we may discuss them in the order which best suits our convenience.

The true hero of *Caesar and Pompey*, as the most cursory reading will show, is Cato, and the epigraph attached to the play, "Only a just man is a free man," is taken from Plutarch's life of him. To make Cato the hero was, of course, to make suicide its subject; for Cato was the type of suicide. The play is almost entirely philosophical; like others in Chapman's later manner, it permits speech to predominate over action. Consequently, when we come to Cato's death, we do not find either the foolish rhapsodies of Fletcher or the guilty conscience of Tourneur; on the contrary we have a logical, reasoned defense of suicide for its own sake (IV, 5; V, 2). Cato is not willing that his life be given to him by Caesar; like some of Chapman's other heroes, his one desire is to be independent and have the control of his actions in his own hands. Hence his death must be in his own hands, too:

> Cato: All just men
> Not only may enlarge their lives, but must,
> From all rule tyrannous, or live unjust.
> *Athenodorus:* By death must they enlarge their lives?
> Cato: By death.
> *Athenodorus:* A man's not bound to that.
> Cato: I'll prove he is.   (IV, 5)

He proceeds to do so, calmly and logically. Man is made for justice and should be as free as justice her-

self; every just man is a law to himself, and therefore

to himself
Is every just man's life subordinate.

Again, the soul is the empress of the body and may
do what she pleases with it, even destroy it when
necessary.

Having reached this point in his argument, Chapman does an interesting thing. He makes the Stoic
Cato produce the Christian notions of the resurrec-
tion of the body and immortality, and argue in
favor of them with considerable eloquence. This is
notable for two reasons: it shows how an original
idea is married to an old one, the revolutionary
being mingled with the conventional; and it proves
(since the arguments for suicide and for immortality are inextricably bound together, and since all
commentators are agreed that the argument for
immortality gives voice to Chapman's own belief)
that the argument for suicide expresses Chapman's
personal conviction. The play is, of course, a Roman play, and the Elizabethans, as we know, were
in the habit of commending suicide in Roman plays;
hence Chapman is not original in putting remarks
favorable to suicide in the mouth of his hero. But
the way his hero expresses himself *is* original. The
other dramatists are either thoughtless or pathetic.
Chapman is neither; his Cato dies in the noblest

fashion, and his suicide is noble because it is the result of careful reasoning carried into action without a qualm. Theory and practice go hand in hand. Cato, we may feel convinced, voices what Chapman himself thought.

In this play, then, we find exemplified the same thing that we found in Donne's *Biathanatos*: one man rises above the general slough of blind acceptance, questioning those beliefs and prejudices which his contemporaries only thoughtlessly repeated. And the dramatist's voice is a far sturdier one than the theologian's; Chapman is much more sure of himself than Donne. Perhaps, being a dramatist, and not having the quibbles of scholars to deal with, he could afford to be.

But Chapman, who was a man of original mind and had a desire to express himself as convincingly as possible, was not content to do so merely in Roman terms. Cato was too remote — the Elizabethans were quite capable of failing to apply to themselves events that took place in 50 B.C. So in *The Revenge of Bussy D'Ambois* he put his notions into modern dress. The hero of this play is Clermont D'Ambois, Bussy's brother, who, like Cato, firmly believes that a just man is a free man, and that a free man is a law unto himself. Clermont is the complete "Senecal" man, whose actions are morally admirable because he entirely controls them. And, his purpose (the avenging of Bussy) accomplished, and his friend the Guise slain, life does not seem worth living (v, 5):

> Since I could skill of man, I never lived
> To please men worldly, and shall I in death,
> Respect their pleasures, making such a jar
> Betwixt my death and life, when death should make
> The consort sweetest, th'end being proof and crown
> To all the skill and worth we truly own?

The Guise is dead, who alone could appreciate true worth:

> None favoring goodness, none but he respecting
> Piety or manhood — shall I here survive,
> Not cast me after him into the sea,
> Rather than here live, ready every hour
> To feed thieves, beasts, and be the slave of power?
> I come, my lord! Clermont, thy creature, comes.

The remark that a good death is the crown of life is one we have frequently heard before. What is startlingly original is its use as the preface to suicide. And let us remember that Clermont, though himself an invention of Chapman's (he is only a vehicle for his creator's Stoic ideas), moved and acted in an environment which was practically contemporary with Chapman's audience; the adventures of Bussy had occurred only about thirty years before.[49] Suicide, in other words, is no longer limited to the restrictions that were formerly put upon it. It is neither committed in Rome nor under the stress of

49. He was murdered on August 15, 1579.

violent emotion; it is the logical and rational end to what, for Chapman, was an ideal existence. The medieval ideas are abandoned, and the Stoic beliefs, which were one of the chief symptoms of the Renaissance, are for the first time in popular literature thoroughly adopted and related to life.[50]

4

The ideas about death in the drama came, as we know, from different sources — from Greece and

50. This defense of suicide may possibly have seemed less striking to the Elizabethans than it does to us. An Elizabethan audience expected the chief character in a tragedy to die in the end, and the dramatists were often careless about motivating such deaths. As Miss Bradbrook points out (*Themes and Conventions of Elizabethan Tragedy*, Cambridge, England, 1935, p. 31), "murder and suicide were committed on the slightest provocation. At the end of a tragedy, in particular, there was no need to discriminate the causes of slaughter. In *Selimus* the physician Abraham takes some of the poison he has administered to the king in a cup of wine, only because

> Faith: I am old as well as Bajazet
> And have not many months to live on earth:
> I care not much to end my life with him —
>
> > (vv. 1829-31)

and in the last act of Rowley's *All's Lost by Lust* one of Antonio's two wives stabs herself with the reflection

> I must die sometime
> And as good die this day as another."

But the language of Miss Bradbrook's first sentence seems to me too strong, as I believe our discussion of suicide has shown, and though her quotations are pertinent to a discussion of Clermont's last speech, they do not lessen the importance of its essential originality. They merely show how Chapman was able to vitalize a flaccid convention by making it the vehicle for his philosophical opinions.

Rome and the Middle Ages — but they were all put into the Elizabethan melting-pot and cooked to various degrees of digestibility. Some were expressed carelessly, some thoughtfully; often the same notion was repeated conventionally by one poet, and originally by another. But there was hardly one which remained unchanged. The Elizabethan dramatists seized on every aspect of death and made each, in one way or another, vividly alive. More than in any other dramatic period death was a fascinating subject for reflection; in this respect the contrast between that time and our own is striking. The Elizabethans enjoyed seeing people die on the stage, they enjoyed being moved by speeches about death, they enjoyed all the situations death produced. Death was much more in their minds than it is in ours, for we have to a large extent forgotten the medieval tradition which was their heritage. Without St. Bernard's contemplation of the sufferings of Christ, and the emphasis on realism that contemplation eventually produced, the late medieval teaching would probably not have existed; and without that teaching, Elizabethan drama would have lost much of its depth, its intensity and richness.

We have only to think of Hamlet to realize how close to the surface the thought of death was. He had been, Ophelia tells us,

> The expectancy and rose of the fair state,
> The glass of fashion and the mould of form;

like the Renaissance as a whole, his "courtier's, soldier's, scholar's eye, tongue, sword" had been ready brilliantly to master the world. But when his view of life was darkened by his mother's marriage and his doubt about his father's murder, external perfection was discarded, and one chief thought took its place. From the beginning of the play to the end, Hamlet thinks of death; his first soliloquy starts with a wish for it, the possibility of suicide haunts him, he feels that earthly things have lost their nobility and their beauty, and he meditates at length upon a skull. Nothing shows more clearly how readily the old ideas could spring to mind, and nothing shows more clearly how they could be transformed into poetry and drama.

Chapter V

THE ELIZABETHAN DRAMA: DRAMATIC
TECHNIQUE

Johnson: "There is no great merit in telling how many
plays have ghosts in them and how this ghost is better
than that. You must shew how terror is impressed on the
human heart."

Boswell's *Life of Johnson*

I

WHEN we turn to the representation of death
on the Elizabethan stage as a part of dramatic technique, we are in a narrower field than
those we have so far been discussing. With one or
two exceptions, the use of death as a dramatic in-
cident has by no means such a many-branched
family tree as have the topics we have just considered. But here as elsewhere, convention, though
within narrower limits, is just as strong, and its use
and development equally worth study.

In our previous discussion we have already
touched on a few of the ways in which matters connected with death were employed for specifically
dramatic purposes. Death himself appears in Kyd's
Soliman and Perseda (above, p. 85); hell is effective
for causing conversion, and thus bringing about the
dénouement (pp. 122 ff.); and the importance of chas-

tity is a common dramatic theme (p. 138). But there are other notions than these which were made useful for the stage.

In our discussion of *Gorboduc* (p. 67) we noticed that there was a dumb-show before the third act: "music of flutes . . . during which came in upon the stage a company of mourners all clad in black, betokening death and sorrow to ensue." This evidently has not the direct symbolic significance of the other dumb-shows in the play. It is used rather for the sake of atmosphere, to give the following action its proper coloring.[1] Marlowe uses black in much the same undeveloped way as the authors of *Gorboduc*: a black flag (*1 Tamb.*, IV, 1) signifying "death and hell" is the signal for the wholesale slaughter of Tamburlaine's enemies.

But though Sackville and Marlowe did not appreciate the possibilities of what they were doing, their successors very shortly did. If a play was to be of serious import, why not give the correct atmosphere at once, and instead of a mourning dumb-show or a black flag, open the play with a funeral

1. See Gascoigne, *Jocasta*, ed. J. W. Cunliffe, Cambridge, England, 1907, vol. 1, p. 261. The second dumb-show:

"Before the beginning of this second act did sound a very doleful noise of flutes: during the which there came in upon the stage two coffins covered with haircloths, and brought in by eight in mourning weed: and accompanied by 8 other mourners: and after they had carried the coffins about the stage, there opened and appeared a Grave, wherein they buried the coffins and put fire to them . . . etc."

procession? The stage directions for Act I, scene 1, of *Titus Andronicus* are as follows: "Enter Martius and Mutius; after two Men bearing a coffin covered with black. . . . The bearers set down the coffin, and Titus speaks." The noisy orange-eating pit is made solemn immediately. *Henry VI*, Part 1, opens in the same fashion. Bedford, Gloucester, and Exeter are standing around the "wooden coffin" of Henry V, glorifying "death's dishonorable victory" with their "stately presence." So Dekker's *Honest Whore* (Part 1) begins: "Enter at one side a Funeral (a coronet lying on the hearse, scutcheon and garlands hanging on the sides)." A funeral procession comes near the beginning of *Richard III* (1, 2); and we are shown the obsequies of Charalois' father at the opening of the second act of Massinger's *Fatal Dowry*. Shakespeare, having used the device in two plays of his own (*Titus Andronicus* and *Richard III*), and having seen it used in a play which he touched up (*Henry VI*), turned it to a more effective purpose in *Hamlet*, where instead of showing us the funeral at the beginning of the play, he waits until the fifth act. He might well have begun the play with the funeral of the old king, and so followed his former practice. It happens, however, that he uses another device with which to start, the suggestion of darkness; and under his treatment it is just as effective as a coffin would be, if not more so. When he does bring in the funeral procession, it appears for the same reason that it would have appeared at the opening: as one of the means to prepare us for the tragic conclusion. Used toward the end in this fashion, it is probably even more successful than when used earlier; one must have seen the play produced in modern setting to realize how moving the mere performance of the funeral ceremony can be.

But this change is not the only "atmospheric" innovation in *Hamlet*. The opening of the fifth act is also, as far as my knowledge goes, the first scene to be laid in a graveyard, and the first scene where skulls are used as stage properties. The effectiveness of this seems to have been at once realized. A short time after the production of *Hamlet*, the first part of *The Honest Whore* appeared (1604), and we there have the skull used much in Shakespeare's way (the play is, indeed, more indebted to Shakespeare than has been generally observed). Hippolito, supposing that Infelice, his lady, has been carried to her grave in the funeral procession we have remarked upon, resolves to spend every Monday meditating

> On nothing but my Infelice's end,
> Or on a dead man's skull draw out mine own.

At the opening of the fourth act, the scene is arranged for this meditation: "Enter a servant," who "sets out a table, on which he places a skull, a picture of Infelice, a book, and a taper." Then Hippolito appears and apostrophizes first the picture, then the skull. To the latter he addresses the following words:

> Perhaps this shrewd pate was mine enemy's:
> 'Las! say it were: I need not fear him now!
> For all his braves, his contumelious breath, [2]
> His frowns, though dagger-pointed, all his plots . . .
> See, see, they're all eaten out! here's not left one!

We may notice in passing one point of interest about Dekker's earlier funeral scene: in a sense it is gratuitous, for the play ends, not in a death, but in a wedding. The creation of an atmosphere of death is not really necessary; it is brought in because it had been proved to be theatrically successful. This type of scene, used previously to announce a tragic conclusion, naturally makes the audience suspect that the play may end tragically. If it does not, at least suspense has been created.

Dekker's use of Shakespeare's innovation was mild compared with what was to come. We have in Tourneur's two tragedies the skull's apotheosis, and, if it does not appear very frequently afterwards, it is probably because Tourneur pushed its use to such an extreme that there seemed nothing more to say about it. *The Revenger's Tragedy* opens with the entrance of Vendice, carrying the skull of his betrothed

---

2. See Hamlet's "The oppressor's wrong, the proud man's contumely," and, for a similarity in tone, his lament over Yorick.

in his hand. With such a beginning no audience could have any doubt as to what sort of play they were going to witness; the atmosphere is created at once. And the skull appears again. The lustful Duke desires Vendice's sister; Vendice promises to procure her. At the rendezvous, however, he appears instead (III, 4) "with the skull of his Betrothed dressed up in tires." In the terrible scene that follows, much of which I shall quote later (p. 238), we have Tourneur's greatest writing. Here if ever are the ordinary remarks about death transformed almost unrecognizably into something vital and new. Vendice poisons the jaws of the skull, the Duke appears, kisses it, and dies. The skull is used for more than the creation of atmosphere; it is the occasion for a stark, ironic poetry to which there are few parallels.

Quite different is the use of the skull in *The Atheist's Tragedy*. Act IV, scene 3, of this play is laid in a churchyard. As the curtain rises the church clock strikes twelve; a charnel house is seen at the back of the stage. Charlemont appears and speaks:

How fit a place for contemplation is this dead of night, among the dwellings of the dead. — This grave — Perhaps the inhabitant was in his life-time the possessor of his own desires. Yet in the midst of all his greatness and his wealth he was less rich and less contented than in this poor piece of earth lower and lesser than a cottage. For here he neither wants nor cares. . . .

The thought we are by this time fully acquainted with; it never found a less convincing expression.

After Charlemont has uttered these remarks an attempt is made to murder him, which fails, and he escapes.   But, he says,

> For more assurance,
> I'll hide me here i' the charnel house,
> This convocation-house of dead men's skulls.
> (*In getting into the charnel house he takes hold of a death's head; it slips, and he staggers.*)
> Death's head, deceivest my hold?
> Such is the trust to all mortality.
> (*Hides himself in the charnel house.*)

Here again we have platitude *qua* platitude. It is an interesting case, for though the expression strikes the reader as flat to a degree, yet, on the stage, with this concrete example before them, it is probable that the people in the audience would have the "trust to all mortality" fairly clearly brought home. The scene advances, and Charlemont rescues Castabella from the atheist's lewd purposes. Together they lie down in the charnel house, "each of them with a death's head for a pillow." Then D'Amville, the atheist, enters "distractedly: he starts at the sight of a death's head"; and after he manifests his distraction, and awakens Castabella and Charlemont, asleep on their bony pillows, the scene ends.

This is atmosphere for atmosphere's sake with a vengeance. Shakespeare, if he saw the play, may well have been surprised at what could be done with his invention.[3] It is certainly a far cry from the modest beginnings in *Gorboduc*.

But *Gorboduc* suggested a further use of the atmosphere of mortality which resembled its source more closely, and which is emotionally even more of a failure than this. It consisted in giving a kind of *post facto* atmosphere, in presenting the circumstances of mourning with reference to what had already happened rather than what was to come. Marston's hero Massinissa (*Sophonisba*, v, 4), after Sophonisba dies, leaves the stage for a moment and returns clad "all in black." So Heywood's Lucrece, after her regrettable experience, is discovered (v, 1) in a room with "a table and a chair covered with black." This device is dramatically feeble: it sacrifices suspense for an obvious theatrical effect in far too easy a fashion. None of the greatest dramatists uses it, and Heywood and Marston only in two of their poorest plays.

I have already pointed out, in speaking of phraseology, how night and darkness were commonly associated with death. Both Shakespeare and Tourneur, as we have seen, used this association for atmospheric purposes — the one in the opening

3. Mr. C. E. Whitmore (*The Supernatural in Tragedy*, Cambridge, Massachusetts, 1915, pp. 245 ff.) considers that Tourneur is here showing himself an "apt pupil of Marston," the Marston of *Antonio's Revenge* and *Sophonisba*. But Marston does not use the skull as Shakespeare and Tourneur do; he is more interested in conjuring up an atmosphere of horror by verbal description.

scene of *Hamlet*, the other in the *Atheist's Tragedy*
(IV, 3). So in the third act of *King Lear*, the night
with all its terrors is used (among the many other
things it is used for) to give the atmosphere of
tragedy. Duncan is murdered late at night (*Macbeth*, II, 1):

> Now o'er the one half-world
> Nature seems dead, and wicked dreams abuse
> The curtain'd sleep; witchcraft celebrates
> Pale Hecate's offerings. . . .

And Marston (again in *Sophonisba*, IV, 1) gives us a
grim picture of night, when

> dark winds,
> Or thick black clouds drive back the blinded stars;

and when Erichtho rises and whispers "dire murmurs" in the throat of the dying man

> which enforce him bear
> Her baneful secrets to the spirits of horror.[4]

---

4. The lines which describe Erichtho's communion with a dead
or dying man are, as Mr. Whitmore says (*op. cit.*, p. 239), "unparalleled in the explicitness with which they detail the loathsomeness of corruption":

> When she finds a corpse
> But newly graved, whose entrails are not turn'd
> To slimy filth, with greedy havoc then
> She makes fierce spoil, and swells with wicked triumph
> To bury her lean knuckles in his eyes;
> Then doth she gnaw the pale and o'ergrown nails
> From his dry hand. . . .

This reminds us of the fifteenth-century funeral monuments, and
was doubtless inspired by a similar taste to that which inspired
them. References to corruption are common enough in the drama,
but there is nothing elsewhere so thoroughgoing as this.

Allied to this practice is the common one of creating the tragic atmosphere, which for the Elizabethans was synonymous with the atmosphere of death, by reference to evil omens. When Macbeth murdered Duncan there were

> Lamentings heard i' the air; strange screams of death,
> And prophesying with accents terrible
> Of dire combustion and confus'd events
> New hatch'd to the woeful time. The obscure bird
> Clamor'd the livelong night: some say the earth
> Was feverous and did shake.

So Bussy D'Ambois (v, 3), before he goes to his death, hears thunder,

> and the frighted earth
> Trembles, and shrinks beneath me; the whole house
> Nods with his shaken burthen.

Romeo (*Romeo and Juliet*, 1, 4), though no physical disturbances occur, dreads "some consequence yet hanging in the stars," and Juliet, as she leans over the balcony to take her last look at him (III, 5), says:

> O God! I have an ill-divining soul:
> Methinks I see thee, now thou art so low,
> As one dead in the bottom of a tomb.

Caesar (*Julius Caesar*, II, 2) is warned by omens not to proceed to the capitol:

> And graves have yawn'd and yielded up their dead
> And ghosts did shriek and squeal about the streets.[5]

---

5. See *Hamlet*, I, 1:
> In the most high and palmy state of Rome
> A little ere the mightiest Julius fell,

This use of omens was an expression of the common superstition that "the heavens themselves blaze forth the death of princes," the desire of the individual to impress himself upon nature, to believe that nature was somehow profoundly interested in him, and when he was threatened with terrible consequences would warn him by terrible manifestations — a desire quite typical of the Renaissance.[6]

Marston, whose use of convention is always illuminating, gives us the best example of this belief; he manages to include in one passage at the beginning of *Antonio's Revenge* (i, 2) almost every kind of omen the Elizabethans were familiar with:

> I tell you, bloods,
> My spirit's heavy, and the juice of life
> Creeps slowly through my stiffen'd arteries.

> The graves stood tenantless and the sheeted dead
> Did squeak and gibber in the Roman streets;
> As stars with trains of fire and dews of blood,
> Disasters in the sun; and the moist star
> Upon whose influence Neptune's empire stands
> Was sick almost to doomsday with eclipse;
> And even the like precurse of fierce events,
> As harbingers preceding still the fates
> And prologue to the omen coming on,
> Have heaven and earth together demonstrated
> Unto our climatures and countrymen.

6. See Painter, *Palace of Pleasure*, ed. J. Jacobs, London, 1890, tom. II, Nov. 23, "Duchess of Malfi":

"The very beastes doe feele some forewarninges [of death], although they see neyther Sworde, nor Staffe, and indevoure to avoyde the cruell Passage of a thynge so Fearefull, as the separation of . . . the body, and Soule."

Last sleep, my sense was steep'd in horrid dreams:
Three parts of night were swallow'd in the gulf
Of ravenous time, when to my slumb'ring powers,
Two meagre ghosts made apparition.
The one's breast seem'd fresh paunch'd with bleeding wounds,
Whose bubbling gore sprang in my frighted eyes;
The other ghost assum'd my father's shape:
Both cried "Revenge!" At which my trembling joints
Icèd quite over with a frozed cold sweat,
Leap'd forth the sheets. Three times I grasp'd at shades,
And thrice, deluded by erroneous sense,
I forc'd my thoughts make stand; when lo, I oped
A large bay window, thorough which the night
Struck terror to my soul. The verge of heaven
Was ring'd with flames, and all the upper vault
Thick-lac'd with flakes of fire; in midst whereof
A blazing comet shot his threat'ning train
Just on my face. Viewing these prodigies,
I bow'd my naked knee and pierc'd the star
With an outfacing eye, pronouncing thus;
Deus imperat astris. At which, my nose straight bled;
Then doubled I my word, so slunk to bed.

Here we have the old superstition that dreams
which come at the end of the night are true; we
have the familiar reference to ghosts and to revenge;
we have quotations from Vergil;[7] darkness is associated with death, the heavens are full of ominous
flames, there is a fatalistic prayer, and, finally, a

---

7. "A frozed cold sweat"; see *Aeneid*, III, 174-175:
        Tum gelidus toto manabat corpore sudor
        Corripio e stratis corpus.
"Three times," etc.; *Aeneid*, VI, 700-701:
        Ter conatus ibi collo dare brachia circum,
        Ter frustra comprensa manus effugit imago.

nose bleed.[8] After all this, an audience could not fail to expect something dreadful to happen. Of course it does, and we may notice that the events which follow depend for their effect almost entirely on surprise; the first part of the play had ended happily enough, and Marston (who, one suspects, could only draw living characters when they reflected his own experiences) needed an external device to make his transition to tragedy convincing. A list of ominous forebodings was the easiest method, and if he overdid the trick, it only shows how available it was.

But this was by no means the only method of creating a deathly atmosphere. In one sense, everything mentioned about the subject helped to create such an atmosphere, but the circumstances of dying, and the objects commonly associated with death, were particularly effective. The owl, "the obscure bird," the "harbinger of death," was frequently used, the church bell was referred to, and the dirge was a not uncommon method of arousing awe.

Valerius, in Heywood's *Rape of Lucrece* (IV, 6), gives us a version of the dirge which shows very well the elements of which it was composed:

8. See Webster, *Duchess of Malfi*, II, 3:

Antonio: My nose bleeds.
　　　　　One that were superstitious would count
　　　　　This ominous, when it merely comes by chance;
　　　　　Two letters, that are wrote here for my name,
　　　　　Are drowned in blood.

Come, list and hark;
   The bell doth toll,
For some but now
   Departing soul.
And was not that
   Some ominous fowl,
The bat, the night-
   Crow or screech-owl?

There is a charming madrigal addressed to the "Sweet Suffolk owl, so richly dight" which expresses the same idea:

Thy note, that forth so freely rolls
With shrill command the mouse controls;
And sings a dirge for dying souls,
   Te whit, te whoo!   Te whit, te whoo![9]

And Webster's two famous dirges (*White Devil*, v, 4; *Duchess of Malfi*, iv, 2) will occur at once to the reader as being in the same tradition.

Indeed, nothing served the Elizabethan dramatists better than a lyric to give a particular emotional tone to their scenes. Webster's great tragedies are full of terror and madness; in *The White Devil* Cornelia chants of "the friendless bodies of unburied men" "in several forms of distraction"; and, clad like a "tomb-maker," with executioners waiting in the background holding "a coffin, cords, and a bell," Bosola recites to the Duchess of Malfi her desperate funeral song. Shakespeare uses the dirge very differently. Neither in the *Tempest* nor in

9. *Elizabethan Lyrics*, ed. Norman Ault, London, 1925, p. 496.

Cymbeline have we a stark atmosphere; all is romantic, remote from tragedy. Consequently we hear of pearls and sea nymphs, of going home to the quiet inevitability of dust; and our nerves, instead of being twisted one further degree to terror, are soothed and calmed.

The appearance of a ghost was, as everyone knows, another dramatic device which had an immense popularity, for not only did it produce an effect of mystery on the audience, but, partly because its mysteriousness enforced attention, it was also an admirable means for exposition. Its use on the stage was borrowed originally from Seneca, and the literary historian has lavished much attention upon it; his having done so makes it unnecessary for us to treat it fully here. As Mr. Cunliffe remarks, when speaking of the characters Seneca passed on to the Elizabethans, "the most important inheritance of English tragedy in this respect was the Ghost." [10] Its dramatic uses, as we have suggested, are chiefly two. In *The Spanish Tragedy*, the ghost of Andrea is effective for expounding the plot and for

10. *The Influence of Seneca on Elizabethan Tragedy*, London, 1893, p. 44. See also J. A. Symonds, *Shakespere's Predecessors*, London, 1884, p. 240; C. E. Whitmore, *The Supernatural in Tragedy*, Cambridge, Massachusetts, 1915, pp. 203 ff.; and F. L. Lucas, *Seneca and Elizabethan Tragedy*, Cambridge, England, 1922. See also the admirable articles of F. W. Moorman, *Modern Language Review*, 1 (1906), 85 ff., 192 ff.; H. Aukenbrand, *Die Figur des Geistes im Drama der Englischen Renaissance*, Leipzig, 1905; J. Dover Wilson, *What Happens in Hamlet*, Cambridge, England, 1935, pp. 52 ff.

giving the desired atmosphere of tragedy. In *Hamlet* its function is the same, though vastly extended. Shakespeare nowhere more clearly shows his dramatic superiority to his contemporaries than in his treatment of this familiar convention. In *Hamlet* he transforms the

> filthy whining ghost,
> Lapt in some foul sheet or a leather pilch,

into a personality with dignity and a new spiritual and dramatic significance. His success probably gave the ghost a longer dramatic life than it would have had otherwise.[11]

Death was used for further technical reasons beside the creation of atmosphere. We have already mentioned how Tourneur's Vendice (in *The Revenger's Tragedy*) dresses up a skull to represent a living person, and we have remarked on its effectiveness. It was not an uncommon experience for the would-be ravisher to encounter a cold body instead of a warm one. Massinissa, in Marston's *Sophonisba*, has made a vow to surrender the heroine to Scipio, the Roman conqueror. Scipio waits expectantly, but Massinissa, instead of his mistress, enters "all in black," and we are shown "the mournful solemnity of Massinissa's presenting Sophonisba's body."

---

11. Some other plays with ghosts are: *Sophonisba*, v, 1; *Catiline*, i, 1; *Atheist's Tragedy*, ii, 6; *White Devil*, v, 4; *Changeling*, v, 1; *Roman Actor*, v, 1; *Bussy D'Ambois*, v, 1; *Revenge of Bussy D'Ambois*, v, 1; *Julius Caesar*, iv, 3, *Macbeth*, iii, 4.

The scene happens to be a failure, but in the hands of other dramatists, who treated the situation more in Tourneur's fashion, it had better success. Shirley uses it in *The Traitor* (v, 3); the Duke desires to enjoy Amidea, and Sciarrha, her brother, promises to arrange matters so that his desire may be accomplished. The curtain rises, "the body of Amidea discovered on a bed, prepared by two gentlewomen." The Duke goes up to her and kisses the corpse:

> What winter dwells
> Upon this lip! 'twas no warm kiss; I'll try
> Again — (*kisses it again*) — the snow is not so cold; I have
> Drunk ice, and feel a numbness spread through all
> My blood at once. — Ha! let me examine
> A little better; Amidea! she is dead, she is dead!

A similar use of the corpse occurs quite early in the history of Elizabethan drama. Tamburlaine, it will be remembered, took Zenocrate's embalmed body around with him to persuade himself she was still alive. But it was Massinger who pushed this dreadful convention to its limits. Sforza, the Duke of Milan, believing her to have been unfaithful to him, has killed his wife Marcelia, whom he passionately adored (*Duke of Milan*, IV, 3). When he discovers that she is innocent, he goes mad, and his madness takes the form of believing that she is still alive, though very ill. Francesco, the villain, appears disguised as a Jewish doctor, and, on his claiming that he can cure Marcelia, the Duke leaves him alone with her. Francesco rouges the cheeks of the body and its lips; his words, as he does so, are horrible. Then the Duke enters, and approaches his dead wife:

> This hand seems as it was when first I kissed it,
> These lips invite too: I could ever feed
> Upon these roses, they still keep their color
> And native sweetness.   (v, 2)

One imagines that this scene presented on the modern stage would be intolerable.[12]

Another fairly common convention was less gruesome and more legitimately effective. For example, in the *Duchess of Malfi* (iv, 2) the Duchess is strangled by Bosola's accomplices and is apparently dead. But after her brother has viewed the supposed corpse, and while Bosola is reproaching himself bitterly for his deed, she revives, speaks a word or two, and then falls back, this time dead in fact. The device naturally aroused great suspense and was taken advantage of by other dramatists beside Webster. Shakespeare had employed it in *Othello* (v, 2); Desdemona, smothered by Othello, lies "still as the grave," but when Emilia enters she revives and says, "O! falsely, falsely murder'd," and exonerates Othello before she dies in reality. Mar-

12. *The Duke of Milan* was given at Merton College, Oxford, in 1924, and I am told that Sir Nigel Playfair, who directed the production, recognized the horror of this scene and tried to tone down its effect by having soft music played while Francesco rouged the cheeks of Marcelia.

ston uses this convention in the *Malcontent* (ii, 3); the Duke thinks he has killed Ferneze, whom he has caught in a compromising situation with the Duchess. But after the Duke has disappeared, Ferneze revives and is brought back to health. Aspasia, in the *Maid's Tragedy* (v, 4), like the Duchess of Malfi, recovers consciousness after her apparent death, only to die in the end.

King Lear illustrates the most striking use of this device, when at the end of the fifth act Lear enters "with Cordelia dead in his arms." Shakespeare plays upon the suspense of the audience with the utmost skill, and we, like Lear himself, are agonized into hoping that Cordelia is still alive.

> She's gone for ever.
> I know when one is dead, and when one lives;
> She's dead as earth.   Lend me a looking glass;
> If that her breath will mist or stain the stone,
> Why, then she lives. . . .
> This feather stirs; she lives! if it be so,
> It is a chance which does redeem all sorrows
> That ever I have felt. . . .
> A plague upon you, murderers, traitors all!
> I might have sav'd her; now, she's gone for ever!
> Cordelia, Cordelia! stay a little.   Ha!
> What is't thou sayst?   Her voice was ever soft,
> Gentle and low, an excellent thing in woman.

Once more a convention has been taken as the basis for dramatic action and exalted into poetry. We hope that Cordelia lives not only because it seems unbearable that she should be dead, but also because, in other plays, the heroine had, at the last moment, come unexpectedly to life, and we think that Cordelia may do the same thing. But she does not, and we realize that Lear, like ourselves, is fooled by his desire. But though our illusion soon fades, his lasts to the end; that is why his final words, still based on this convention, are poignant almost beyond expression:

> Do you see this? Look on her, look, her lips,
> Look there, look there!

The most interesting use of death as a part of dramatic technique (if it is correct so to classify it) is the part it plays in the exhibition of character. The brave man, the hero, dies gladly, scorning to fear; the coward dies trembling. Bravery in front of death is a characteristic of nearly all the chief heroes of Elizabethan drama. So much was it expected by the audience that sometimes a dramatist was forced to make his hero inconsistent in order to satisfy the demand. As we shall see, this is true of both Marlowe's Tamburlane and Chapman's Byron.

It has always been a common convention. In the Middle Ages the saints' legends had established a routine to be followed by all who wanted to die well: the individual made a final speech, commended his soul to the hands of his God, and was carried by angels to heaven. And not only in the Middle Ages but throughout the time of the fullest

dramatic activity, much emphasis was placed on
the way a person died; the day of death was the
day which "judged all others:" we must not forget
that Foxe's *Book of Martyrs* was in all Elizabethan
libraries. We should therefore expect to find in
the drama that the way a person dies throws light
on his character; we still feel today that a man
who bravely faces his end is a man to be admired.
It is a natural belief, and it has always had high
literary value.

But scholars have not been content to leave the
matter here. Not recognizing either the universal
feeling about a man's last moments or the fact
that it had been fully expressed in all previous literature, they have been determined to seek a specific
source for the Elizabethan emphasis on bravery.
The characters of Seneca despise death and die
nobly; therefore when an Elizabethan character
does the same thing, he must be imitating the heroes
of Seneca.[13] It is by no means necessary to make
this assumption. It may possibly be true that the
Duchess of Malfi would not have cried, as a refuge
against annihilation, "I am Duchess of Malfi
still" if Seneca's Medea had not exclaimed, "Medea
superest"; and it may also be true that Stoical sentiments in the mouths of dying characters are a
remnant of Seneca's influence; but that the scorn

13. See Cunliffe, *The Influence of Seneca on Elizabethan Tragedy*,
London, 1893, pp. 29 ff.

of death which so many stage Elizabethans show is purely the result of reading Seneca, I find it difficult to believe. If further evidence than that of human nature be required, numerous examples of noble deaths may be produced from sixteenth-century non-dramatic literature.[14]

Even the Stoicism which is considered so Senecan may be found in works which, to my knowledge, have never been thought to owe much to Seneca. Albanact, for example, in the *Mirror for Magistrates*, dies in just that attitude of fatalism which has been attributed to Seneca alone (st. 72):

> But what avayles, to strive against the tide . . .
> Sith Nature hath the ende of thinges assin'd,
>   There is no nay, wee must perforce depart,
>   Gainst dinte of death there is no ease by arte.

---

14. See Wm. Painter, *Palace of Pleasure*, ed. J. Jacobs, London, 1890, "Lucrece": "'No unchast or ill woman, shall hereafter impute no dishonest act to Lucrece.' Then she drewe out a knife, which she had hidden secretely, under her kirtle, and stabbed her selfe to the harte." "The piteous and chaste death of one of the muleters wives of the Queene of Navare." This lady died like a medieval saint, a "Marter of chastite." "When . . . she perceived death approch, lifting up her eyes unto heaven, and joyning her hands together, gave thanckes unto God." "Duchess of Malfi": when she dies, she asks her executioners to look after her children, and to have regard for her maid. "'I also recommend unto you' (quod she) 'this pore imprisoned mayden, and entreate hir well, in consideration of hir good service done to the unfortunate Duchesse of Malfi.' As she had ended those words, the two Ruffians did put a coarde about her neck, and strangled hir." See also *Mirror for Magistrates*, ed. J. Haslewood, London, 1815, "Humber"; and the true account of Southwell's death in his *Triumphs over Death*, ed. J. W. Trotman, London, 1914, appendix II.

Such a state of mind is by no means infrequent, and it could be produced equally well by both decaying Rome and the decaying Middle Ages.

There were plenty of noble deaths in real life. Oldys, in his life of Sir Walter Raleigh, describes the execution of his hero: "Having fingered the edge of it [the axe] a little, he returned it and said, smiling to the sheriff, 'This is a sharp medicine, but it is a sound cure for all diseases'" — a remark which, spurious or not, was probably not caused by having read Seneca.

But let us turn to specific dramatic examples. "Doth not death affright you?" Bosola asks the Duchess of Malfi (IV, 2). "Who could be afraid on't," she replies, "knowing to meet such excellent company in the other world?" So Vittoria Corombona (*White Devil*, III, 1) says to her judges:

> Find me but guilty, sever head from body,
> We'll part good friends: I scorn to hold my life
> At yours or any man's entreaty, sir.

In a similar way, Charlemont, the hero of *The Atheist's Tragedy*, faces death (V, 2). He and Castabella stand together on the scaffold, and Castabella speaks for them both: "In scorn of death thus hand in hand we die." "With an active spirit" he aspires "to undergo [his] death"; and though the modern reader cannot help considering him a prig, yet Tourneur doubtless meant his audience to consider his attitude praiseworthy. It is in violent contrast to the attitude of D'Amville, as that atheist realizes:

> This argument of death congeals my blood.
> Cold fear, with apprehension of thy end,
> Hath frozen up the rivers of my veins.

This contrast in the manner of dying was a useful device for the dramatist; it made his characters more vivid by setting them against each other. Webster puts Cariola's frantic struggles for life against the magnificent integrity of the Duchess (*Duchess of Malfi*, IV, 2); the author of *Nero* (to name only one more example out of many) compares Seneca's willingness to die with the Emperor's reluctance.

In fact the importance of dying well was very heavily emphasized. Old Andrugio, in Marston's *Antonio and Mellida* (V, 1), asking about the supposed death of his son Antonio, becomes violent at the slightest suggestion of weakness:

> Did his hand shake, or his eye look dull,
> His thoughts reel fearful when he struck the stroke?
> And if they did, I'll rend them out the hearse,
> Rip up his cerecloth, mangle his bleak face,
> That when he comes to heaven, the powers divine
> Shall ne'er take notice that he was my son.

Not every hero, of course, faces death bravely, not every villain fearfully. Chapman's Duke of Byron protests violently and by every possible means against his execution (*Tragedy of Byron*; v, 4); and the Duke of Guise, in the *Revenge of Bussy D'Ambois* (v, 4), is conscious of the fear of death, though he does his best to overcome it. So Claudio, in *Measure for Measure*, shrinks from the thought of dying, and Hamlet is prevented from suicide by "the fear of something after death." But in these cases, also, their attitude towards death throws light on the speakers' characters; it is more revealing, certainly, with Byron and Claudio, than anything else we know about them.

The last dramatic tradition we shall consider — the speeches put into the mouths of those who die — is connected with this one. There were several conventions associated with this, by far the most common being that which turned a dying man's last words into a couplet. This awkward custom was perhaps the result of the belief in the importance of the last words spoken:

> O! but they say the tongues of dying men
> Enforce attention like deep harmony — [15]

and weighty moral speeches were usually put in rhyme. More probably the custom arose from the fact that couplets were used in Elizabethan drama to end a scene, and a scene very frequently ended with a death. Whatever the cause, more than half the characters of Elizabethan tragedy greet death with a rhyme. Dorothea's last words (*Virgin Martyr*,

15. *Richard II*, ii, 1.

IV, 3) are merely representative of a very popular tradition:

> Say this of Dorothea, with wet eyes,
> "She lived a virgin, and a virgin dies."

Nearly all the couplets are as fatuous as this. Even Othello dies with what seems to a modern reader an artificial comment:

> I kiss'd thee ere I kill'd thee; no way but this,
> Killing myself to die upon a kiss.

But in Shakespeare Othello is an exception; the dying speeches of his other tragic heroes are magnificent, and Othello himself, before he speaks this couplet, has superbly taken farewell of the world. The last words of Hamlet and Antony vibrate unforgettably in our minds; in poetry Shakespeare's heroes and heroines transcend and transfigure death, as in a sense they transcend personality. The convention which made Shakespeare emphasize their final utterance is from one point of view defeated by his genius.

Othello's couplet brings us to another conventional way of dying. Romeo says, "Thus, with a kiss, I die"; Mrs. Frankford in *A Woman Killed with Kindness* asks her husband for another kiss before she departs: "Once more: thy wife dies thus embracing thee." So Sophonisba expires

> Secure from bondage and all servile harms,
> But more, — most happy in my husband's arms.

Shirley's Amidea (*Traitor*, v, 1) will not waste the short time left her in embraces: "Kiss me when I am dead," she says, "You else will stay my journey." This is unusual; little Hengo in Fletcher's *Bonduca* (v, 5) dies like Mrs. Frankford, saying: "Kiss me: so, Farewell, farewell!"

This speech leads us on to another common way of dying, which is, after all, obvious enough. One was leaving the world, what more natural than to say "farewell"? "O Rome, farewell!" cries Nero (*Nero*, v, 3). "Commend me to my kind lord. O! farewell!" says Desdemona, and dies.[16]

On the other hand, particularly in the earlier plays, many characters die without saying anything at all. Many, like Shakespeare's Antony, die while someone else is talking; sometimes death overtakes a character, as it does Hotspur, in the middle of a sentence. But these are minor points, and we need not spend our time on them.

Thus, though they are neither as varied nor as interesting as the verbal and moral conventions, there were a large number of technical devices used on the Elizabethan stage in relation to death. Like

16. See *Mirror for Magistrates*, ed. J. Haslewood, London, 1815, "Albanact," st. 70:
> Farewell, farewell, to mourne will not prevayle,
> I see with Knife where *Atropos* doth stand;
> Farewell, my friendes, my children and my land,
>   And farewell all my subjectes, farewell breath,
>   Farewell ten thowsand times, and welcome death.

everything else worked on the Elizabethan anvil, death became welded into dramatic form. Funeral processions, skulls, omens, all the inherited superstitions, were employed to make the plays effective. And it is clear how communal the great majority of these conventions and superstitions were; they lay at the back of everybody's mind. The dramatist may, in many cases, have used them subconsciously (one of the benefits of tradition is that it allows the subconscious safely to take the upper hand); but however they were drawn upon, once they appeared in a play they were sure to be recognized by the audience. In their common possession of these traditions the dramatist and his audience were one.

2

It will be illuminating to bring this chapter to a close in the same way in which we began our discussion of the drama in Chapter III: with a reference to a single play. For this purpose I have chosen Fletcher's *Bonduca*, although almost any other would do as well. *Bonduca*, however, has the advantage of being an original production, for its source is a passage of only a few lines in Tacitus' *Annals*. Thus the author put into the story whatever remarks he saw fit, and he was at liberty to invent (i.e. to draw on the contents of his mind) as he pleased. I have also chosen this play because it is fairly late in date, and hence represents the final tendencies of the Elizabethan drama. It was produced about 1614, fifty-three years after *Gorboduc*.

The plot may be outlined as follows: Bonduca and her brother-in-law, Caratach, are defending Britain against the Roman forces, led by Suetonius. In a great battle they are defeated, and Bonduca and her two daughters, rather than fall into Roman hands, commit suicide. At this battle, however, the Romans are not present in full force; Poenius, a Roman captain, has not appeared because he is doubtful of the issue. Therefore when he hears the news of the victory he also kills himself. Caratach, the British chieftain, has escaped from the battle with his little nephew, Hengo, and he is sought after anxiously by the Romans. With Hengo he has taken refuge on the top of a rock, but at last he is discovered. Hengo is killed by an arrow, and Caratach is led off to captivity.

The first remark about death occurs in the second scene of Act I. Suetonius is conversing with his captains; one of them, Petillius, is describing the danger that awaits the Roman army. Suetonius reassures him:

Suetonius: These are imaginations, dreams of nothings:
The man that doubts or fears —
Decius: I am free of both.
Demetrius: The self-same I.
Petillius: And I as free as any;
As careless of my flesh, of that we call life,
So I may lose it nobly, as indifferent
As if it were my diet.

To realize how unoriginal these sentiments are, we have only to remember what has .been said about the nobility of a soldier's death, the desire for fame, and the importance of a brave facing of death for the establishment of a favorable impression.

At the beginning of the second act we are introduced to Poenius, the captain who is later to commit suicide. He is now making his fatal decision not to join his general in an attack on the Britons:

> Who but fools,
> That make no difference betwixt certain dying
> And dying well, would fling their fames and fortunes
> Into this Britain-gulf, this quick-sand-ruin,
> That, sinking, swallows us?

And as we hear his words, we are reminded of all the other occasions on which the importance of a good death is emphasized, of Montaigne, of the Thane of Cawdor, in whose life "nothing so well became him as the leaving of it," and of many other characters who are admirable because they died bravely.

The battle soon takes place (III, 5), and the renegade Poenius, standing at a distance, describes it for us:

> Death rides in triumph, Drusus, fell Destruction
> Lashes his fiery horse, and round about him
> His many thousand ways to let out souls.

His words, also, call up many former recollections, perhaps of the impersonation of death in the

Apocalypse, certainly (in the terms with which destruction is described) of the adjective Shakespeare used of the "fell sergeant"; and, in the last line, one remembers that Poenius is here repeating what Vergil, Seneca, Montaigne, Sidney, Webster, and others had said before him, and what Ford was to say again.

After the battle, Caratach escapes with his nephew on his back (IV, 2) and the following conversation occurs. It strikes us as familiar:

Caratach: How does my boy?
  Hengo: I would do well; my heart's well;
        I do not fear.
Caratach: My good boy!
  Hengo: I know, uncle,
        We must all die; my little brother died,
        I saw him die, and he died smiling; sure,
        There's no great pain in't, uncle.   But, pray, tell me,
        Whither must we go when we are dead?
Caratach: (*aside*) Strange questions! —

a comment with which the reader is hardly likely to agree. The scene continues in this fashion for some time; Fletcher makes the most of little Hengo, as we shall shortly discover.

In the next scene we are shown the ashamed and remorseful Poenius; the Romans have been victorious, and he was afraid to join them; there is nothing left but suicide.

> I am only thinking now, sir,
> (For I am resolved to go) of a most base death,
> Fitting the baseness of my fault.   I'll hang.

He is discouraged from this, however:

> Your sword must do the deed:
> 'Tis shame to die choked, fame to die and bleed —

words which surely offer a capital example of an
undigested truism, the unconsidered repetition of a
convention we are by now fully familiar with.
These words persuade Poenius. He exclaims:

> Heavens,
> Ye everlasting powers, I am yours! (*falls upon his sword*)
> The work's done,
> That neither fire, nor age, nor melting envy,
> Shall ever conquer. Carry my last words
> To the great general: kiss his hands, and say,
> My soul I give to Heaven, my fault to justice. . . .
> I die:
> Lie lightly on my ashes, gentle earth!

Here again we are on familiar ground; but there
is a quality in this speech which is lacking in the
lines immediately preceding it. The words are a
little more genuine; Fletcher seems to have felt the
situation and been moved by it. The old ideas about
the significance of last words, the ascent to heaven,
the brave death, the request that earth lie lightly,[17]
are here, but they are given a slightly fresh color
and made faintly alive, as the others are not. The

---

17. This was so common on Roman grave-stones that frequently
only the initials were printed: S. T. T. L. (sit tibi terra levis).
See Northcote, *Epitaphs of the Catacombs*, and the well-known song in
The Maid's Tragedy, ending,

> Upon my buried body lie
> Lightly, gentle earth.

passage is not memorable poetry, but it is effective drama.

In the fourth scene of the same act (IV) we are shown the end of Bonduca and her daughters. At the beginning of the scene Bonduca sends Nennius, one of her commanders, on an errand which is sure to cause his death. As he goes, Bonduca remarks, in words whose like we have heard before:

> Farewell, with all my heart! we shall meet yonder,
> Where few of these must come.

Then, in sight of the Romans, Bonduca and her daughters prepare to commit suicide. The second daughter is, however, afraid to die: "Oh, gentle mother! . . . Oh, my heart! I dare not." Her sister encourages her: "Do it, worthy sister; 'Tis nothing; 'tis a pleasure: We'll go with you." To which the second daughter replies, "Oh, if I knew but whither!" The first daughter gives a brief description of the delights of heaven:

> *Second daughter:* That steels me;
> A long farewell to this world!

And she stabs herself and dies. Then the first daughter follows her example:

> Would ye learn
> How to die bravely, Romans, to fling off
> This case of flesh, lose all your cares for ever? . . .
> Keep your minds humble, your devotions high;
> So shall ye learn the noblest part, to die.

Then it is Bonduca's turn. She drinks poison, and
addresses the Romans:

> Ye fools;
> Ye should have tied up Death first, when ye conquered;
> Ye sweat for us in vain else: see him here!
> He's ours still, and our friend; laughs at your pities;
> And we command him with as easy reins
> As do our enemies.

And so she dies, on a couplet as usual:

> If you will keep your laws and empire whole,
> Place in your Roman flesh a Briton soul.

Only little Hengo remains. His death is prepared for in a manner with which we are now fully
acquainted. In Act v, scene 1, Caratach appears
with his nephew. When they have talked for a moment, a soft dead march is heard within, and
shortly afterward a funeral procession arrives. It
turns out to be that of Poenius, his coffin borne by
soldiers. Caratach approaches it, and asks that the
hearse be set down so that he may "lend a tear to
virtue." He then apostrophizes the body:

> Sleep peaceably;
> Happiness crown thy soul, and in thy earth
> Some laurel fix his seat, there grow and flourish,
> And make thy grave an everlasting triumph!

The last scene of the play, prepared for by this
atmosphere, shows Hengo and Caratach on their
rock, faint from hunger. A Roman with the significant name of Judas has discovered them, and he

places as bait a basket of food at the bottom of the
rock. They notice this, and Caratach lowers Hengo
down by the belt to get it. This gives Judas his opportunity, and he shoots Hengo with an arrow.
Caratach draws him up again, having crushed
Judas' skull with a stone, and finds that his nephew
is mortally wounded.

Hengo: Oh, I bleed hard! I faint too; out upon't
How sick I am! — The lean rogue, uncle!

Caratach: Look, boy;
I have laid him sure enough. . . .

Hengo: Hold my sides hard; stop, stop; oh, wretched fortune,
Must we part thus? Still I grow sicker, uncle. . . .

Caratach: Oh, my chicken,
My dear boy, what shall I lose?

Hengo: Why, a child,
That must have died however; had this scaped me,
Fever or famine — I was born to die, sir.

Caratach: But thus unblown, my boy?

Hengo: I go the straighter
My journey to the gods. . . .
Pray for me;
And, noble uncle, when my bones are ashes,
Think of your little nephew! — Mercy!

Caratach: Mercy!
You blessèd angels, take him!

Hengo: Kiss me: so,
Farewell, farewell (*dies*)!

Caratach: . . . Time and Death,
Ye have done your worst.

There is here hardly an observation which is new.
In fact, the whole play, as far as death is concerned,
is a collection of conventions, used, to be sure, ap-

propriately enough, but rarely with sufficient conviction to be turned into poetry. That is why *Bonduca* is significant, for it shows the conventions in
their every day form, unvitalized by the intensity
with which greater poets than Fletcher were able
infuse them. Fletcher, it is true, seems to have
had a limited range of feelings about death (wider,
however, than Ben Jonson's, in whose plays there
are virtually no remarks on the subject[18]) and as
a result, though he often refers to death, he relies on the communal phrases, ideas, and devices
more literally than did his superiors. But if we
compare his use of these conventions with the manner in which they were employed in *Gorboduc* we

18. This fact is worth a moment's attention, for it emphasizes
the difference between Jonson's drama and that of his contemporaries. Only very rarely in his work can we find expressions of those
common feelings about common facts which are part of the Elizabethan dramatic background. His work, as Mr. T. S. Eliot has
pointed out in an illuminating essay, is "of the surface." And no
matter how solid that surface may be made (as Eliot remarks,
Jonson's surface, the kind of life he creates, is constructed with
great firmness), it is not the same thing as the poetry of Webster
or Tourneur or Shakespeare. Jonson deliberately set out to
"sport with human follies, not with crimes," and we do not expect
to find in his humors comedies those emotional roots which make
the greatest Elizabethan plays so moving. But his tragedies have
not those roots either; that is why *Sejanus* and *Catiline* are bloodless.
By the *kind* of artistic self-consciousness Jonson used, he cut himself
off from one of the main emotional arteries of his age, and it is a
curious paradox, involving, perhaps, the need for a redefinition of
critical terms, that the foremost classicist of his time should have
proved the dangers of individualism by being himself too great an
individualist.

find that in *Bonduca* the conventions are far more effective for the stage. Instead of a dumb-show we have a funeral procession accompanied by long emotive speeches; Bonduca and her daughters, in a halo of fine sentiments, commit suicide in front of the audience — quite a different affair from the death of Gorboduc and his sons behind the scenes.

There is thus a great change in the dramatic treatment of death between 1561 and 1614. What was rhetorical in *Gorboduc* becomes emotional in *Bonduca*; what is sentiment in *Bonduca* was only statement in *Gorboduc*. In this *Bonduca* is representative of all the Elizabethan drama; and it is worth noticing, as we look back on our discussion, how large a variety of emotion was aroused by the different ways the dramatists handled death. Seneca's device of describing death-bed scenes by means of narrative could, of course, be successful enough, but it had two chief difficulties: it was limited, and it was monotonous. The messenger could arouse pity and fear by his story of death, but those emotions were framed by the terms of his recital; the audience was at one remove from the events described, and since they were events that had already happened, they had no immediacy, and did not affect the listener as they would had he been a spectator as well. And once he had heard one of these descriptions, he had heard them all; it is diffi-cult to vary the narrative of a dying scene, and if the device is used more than two or three times by a playwright of mediocre talent (like Seneca) the audience becomes bored. This is particularly true if the audience is, for the most part, standing on its feet instead of reclining on comfortable couches. Furthermore the medieval tradition of play-writing made the Elizabethan spectators expect to see everything acted out before them, and I do not believe that any play with much narrative in it had a popular success on the later Elizabethan stage.[19]

Hence it was almost inevitable that the lively minds of the Elizabethan dramatists should neglect this worn-out convention, and by showing the deaths of their characters actually on the stage should give themselves a much wider emotional range. We have noticed many examples of the different kinds of death-bed scenes; each playwright of ability seems to have had one type of emotion upon which he continually played. Marlowe's heroes protest violently against death, and we share their anger and their shaken pride; Fletcher's people speak about death as if it were something gently soothing, and it is only after we have been temporarily lulled into a soft melancholy that we become aware that the whole thing is overdone. Webster probes our emotions more

19. *Bussy D'Ambois* is a possible exception, but even here there is only one narrative speech of any length.

deeply, and, with Flamineo and Bosola, we feel that death is merely the final bitterness of a life without moral values, against whose meaningless horror we can only defend ourselves with a wry and mocking joke. The almost unbearable pathos of the death of Lear, the bravado of Othello, the frenzy of Chapman's Byron, all these and many other varieties of emotion would have been impossible had not the Senecan shackles been broken. And that they should have been broken was inevitable, for there was a more immediate tradition than that of Seneca, a tradition that had deeper roots in men's thoughts and feelings. Without the late medieval emphasis on death these great scenes, the glory of Elizabethan drama, would in all probability never have been written.

But the emotions such scenes arouse are interesting not only for their variety and intensity; they have, if we examine them closely, a definite connection with each other which is of much importance for a true understanding of the Elizabethan mind. What this connection is, how it came about, and what it implies, are the questions which finally demand our attention.

Chapter VI

THE DRAMA AND THE RENAISSANCE MIND

> *Capuchin:* Pray tell me, do not you meditate of death?
> *Romelio:* Phew, I took out that lesson,
>   When I once lay sick of an ague: I do now
>   Labor for life, for life!
>
>   Webster, *The Devil's Law-Case*

I

WE HAVE now seen how rich and elaborate was the Elizabethan dramatic treatment of death, and we may consider the conventions so far studied as the basis of Elizabethan opinion on the subject. The words, the ideas, the technical devices, were all common property, and, as a result of their use by the various dramatists, they were re-vitalized and given new form. In *Gorboduc*, as we know, the remarks which were current about death in nearly all sixteenth-century literature were repeated, much as they had appeared in lyrics and versified narratives. *Gorboduc* is itself little more than a narrative spoken by different people, and hence the phrases had little opportunity to be reborn. But as the drama developed, and Senecan oratory gave way to Elizabethan action, these phrases and ideas stopped being mere ornaments and became vivid dramatic actualities. Thought about death was no longer expressed in a set of lifeless platitudes but in images that caught the mind of the spectator and made him feel, with the actor, the emotions the dramatist had put into his characters.

But a study of death and the Elizabethans must do more than point out such facts as these. What must now occupy us is a chronological history of the attitude toward death expressed in the drama; we must find out how, in the generation or two we have been discussing, the conventions inherited from the Middle Ages and the sixteenth-century conflict were changed by the individual dramatists; we must decide whether a different point of view from that of the past was developed and if, once it had developed, it remained.

We have already seen how the non-dramatic literature of the sixteenth century reflected the two opposing attitudes to life which were to be found in that time. No conclusion was arrived at; this world and the next were valued by their partisans unreflectingly, and Montaigne was almost alone in the serious expression of new ideas. When people were forced to think of death, they thought in a medieval way; the early Elizabethan enthusiasm about life was in this respect almost entirely inarticulate.

We find an interesting reflection of this in many early plays, where the hero, as he is about to die, has nothing whatever to say. In *Arden of Feversham* (v, 1) the hero dies silently as his various assailants stab him. When Absolon is killed (*David and Bethsabe*, sc. 13), though he protests against his murder, we have only the stage direction, "they stab him; he dies"; the victim himself is silent. In *The Spanish Tragedy*, in spite of many remarks about hell and revenge, the final catastrophe (iv, 4) occurs with the chief characters speechless; Hieronimo naturally says nothing (he has bitten out his tongue), and the Duke falls heavily without a word. *Titus Andronicus* shows the same thing (v, 3):

> *Titus:* 'Tis true, 'tis true; witness my knife's sharp point
> (*kills Tamora*).
> *Saturninus:* Die, frantic wretch, for this accursed deed
> (*kills Titus*)!
> *Lucius:* Can the son's eye behold his father bleed?
> There's meed for meed, death for a deadly deed
> (*kills Saturninus*)!

Before the time of Marlowe the playwrights had not yet learned how to make the death of a hero effective on the stage, and in not having done so they accurately reflected their time.

It was Marlowe who first discovered how to use death dramatically, for he realized that the manner in which a character acts at the moment of death throws an emotional light on his personality which can be obtained in no other way. Furthermore, in the type of hero he invented he first gave expression to that conflict between two views of life and death which may justly be considered a possible cause for the greatness of the Elizabethan drama.

The theme of *Tamburlaine* is material conquest. Tamburlaine sets out to master the earth, to put under his subjection the monarchs of Asia and Europe, and to be made "famous through the world" (Part 1, iii, 3). He comes very near to accomplishing his aim; he is successful in all his battles, and apparently in all he sets his heart on. But there is one force he cannot conquer, and just as Tamburlaine's own ambition is of all ambitions the most material and earthly, so his opponent is the simplest and most fundamental of earthly enemies — death. It is by the fatal illness of his beloved Zenocrate that Tamburlaine first becomes aware of his opponent (Part 2, ii, 4).

Tamburlaine: Tell me, how fares my fair Zenocrate?
  Zenocrate: I fare, my lord, as other empresses,
      That, when this frail and transitory flesh
      Hath sucked the measure of that vital air
      That feeds the body with his dated health,
      Wanes with enforced and necessary change.
Tamburlaine: May never such a change transform my love,
      In whose sweet being I repose my life,
      Whose heavenly presence, beautified with health,
      Gives light to Phoebus and the fixed stars.

He cannot face Zenocrate's death, though Zenocrate herself submits to it uncomplainingly. And when she does die, Tamburlaine's fury is boundless:

  What, is she dead? Techelles, draw thy sword,
  And wound the earth, that it may cleave in twain,
  And we descend into th' infernal vaults,
  To hale the fatal Sisters by the hair,

And throw them in the triple moat of hell,
For taking hence my fair Zenocrate.
Casane and Theridamas, to arms!
Raise cavalieros higher than the clouds,
And with the cannon break the frame of heaven;
Batter the shining palace of the sun,
And shiver all the starry firmament. . . .
Behold me here, divine Zenocrate,
Raving, impatient, desperate, and mad,
Breaking my steeled lance, with which I burst
The rusty beams of Janus' temple doors,
Letting out death and tyrannising war.

This is more than mere rant; it expresses the child-like character of the Scythian conqueror, frustrated for the first time. That death should oppose him is something he cannot understand; previously it had always been his servant:

Tamburlaine: Behold my sword; what see you at the point?
  1st Virgin: Nothing but fear and fatal steel, my lord.
Tamburlaine: Your fearful minds are thick and misty, then,
        For there sits Death; there sits imperious Death,
        Keeping his circuit by the slicing edge.

                            (Part 1, v, 2)

But now death, not Tamburlaine, is the master; and its suddenly turning against him is a thing that Tamburlaine will neither comprehend nor submit to. As a result he orders Zenocrate's body to be embalmed, and carries it about with him for the rest of his life.

But the time comes, of course, when death is not willing to allow even this hollow victory, and so turns against Tamburlaine himself. At first Tamburlaine is less than ever willing to be reconciled (Part 2, v, 3):

> What daring god torments my body thus,
> And seeks to conquer mighty Tamburlaine?
> Shall sickness prove me now to be a man,
> That have been term'd the terror of the world? . . .
> Come, let us march against the powers of heaven,
> And set black streamers in the firmament,
> To signify the slaughter of the gods.

He will attack Atlas — "whose shoulders bear the axis of the world" — so that with his own death, heaven and earth will perish too. But suddenly a change seems to come over him and he recognizes that he must die after all:

> No, for I shall die.
> See, where my slave, the ugly monster death,
> Shaking and quivering, pale and wan for fear,
> Who flies away at every glance I give,
> And, when I look away, comes stealing on!

The doctors pronounce Tamburlaine to be seriously ill, and he sends for a map to review his conquests, noting how large a part of the earth is yet to be conquered by his sons. Then Amyras is crowned as his successor; Tamburlaine commands that the body of Zenocrate be put beside him; he dismisses the thought that he may survive:

> Casane, no; the monarch of the earth,
> And eyeless monster that torments my soul,
> Cannot behold the tears ye shed for me,
> And therefore still augments his cruelty.

And finally, bidding farewell, he falls back lifeless. "For Tamburlaine, the scourge of God, must die."

Here, for the first time, death is treated dramatically. To begin with, through his use of language Marlowe personifies death more vividly than any dramatist had done before, so that we see the eyeless monster, as Tamburlaine sees him, standing before us. In the second place he describes a hero's reaction to death as an indication of character. And in the third place, he seems to be aware that death can be employed in the drama to give wider implications to the action than would otherwise be possible. Tamburlaine's death is not the violent kind he is familiar with; it is an extinction of life by the more subtle and common enemy of disease; a material ambition meets a material defeat. As we read the play we feel that Marlowe has broadened the scope of Tamburlaine's story, has given it, partly through his treatment of death, a philosophical and universal meaning. It is more than a dramatized series of adventures; it is an expression of Marlowe's age, and Tamburlaine is a type of all conquerors. For these reasons, the debt that the later drama owes to Marlowe is incalculable. He gave the drama "high seriousness," not only by his use of a nobler verse than any of his predecessors could manage, but also by an insight, a comprehension, of which that verse was an expression. Without him the wide range of emotion about death, and about life, which the later dramatists were able to master would perhaps have been impossible. And in our recognition of this fact we must overlook the somewhat confused way in which the death of Tamburlaine is described; Marlowe does not successfully combine his conception of Tamburlaine's character with the convention that demanded the brave death of a hero; it is too much to expect that he could have achieved completion at once. It was enough to have started the Elizabethan drama on its magnificent career, and to have expressed so well the attitude toward life which was shared by most of his contemporaries. For to the early English Renaissance, as to Tamburlaine, this world alone mattered, and death was tragic in that it brought worldly glory to a close.

In *Faustus* the problem is carried further. *Faustus* is also a play on the theme of power, but instead of seeking, like Tamburlaine, mere territorial conquest, Faustus wishes to be master of the supernatural. Here, far more obviously than in *Tamburlaine*, the Renaissance discusses its own chief problem, and the conflict with the past is made definitely vocal. In *Tamburlaine* the question of value had not arisen; here it does arise. The present world is set against the next, the Renaissance against the Middle Ages.

The play is well known, but it will make our discussion clearer to outline it once again. Dr. Faustus sells his soul to Mephistophilis in return for twenty-four years' enjoyment of beauty, wealth, learning, and power; he says:

> I'll be great Emperor of the world,
> And make a bridge thorough the moving air,
> To pass the ocean with a band of men;
> I'll join the hills that bind the Afric shore,
> And make that country continent to Spain,
> And both contributory to my crown.

He is given one book wherein he may "see all characters and planets of the heavens," and another wherein are shown "all plants, herbs, and trees that grow upon the earth." He,

> To know the secrets of astronomy,
> Graven in the book of Jove's high firmament,
> Did mount himself to scale Olympus' top;

he makes visible the greatest conqueror of the antique world; he hears its greatest love story sung by its greatest poet:

> Have I not made blind Homer sing to me
> Of Alexander's love and Œnon's death?
> And hath not he that built the walls of Thebes
> With ravishing sound of his melodious harp,
> Made music with my Mephistophilis?

And finally, he has Helen of Troy for his paramour. In other words, he obtains all that the Renaissance desired. Marlowe meant him to lack nothing, though the magnitude of his achievements is not well emphasized. It is not emphasized because Marlowe was interested in something else: in showing that all these things are valueless compared with the security of Faustus' soul. Faustus dies in torment; the devils carry him off to hell. His death, in medieval phrase, is the gate to eternal life. In all his last speech there is not one expression of regret about leaving the pleasures he has enjoyed for the past twenty-four years. His whole mind is concentrated on the future world, he thinks of nothing but of the tortures awaiting him, and he prays, not for a continuance of life, but for an ascent to heaven.

Hence we may say that at the beginning of the drama's interest in death, the medieval point of view conquered. Marlowe, like Nashe in *Christs Teares*, though he wrote with the linguistic brilliance and wealth of the Renaissance, expressed an opinion thoroughly in accord with that of the fourteenth century. The view of death which Christianity had taught for the past twelve hundred years was still triumphant; and the English Renaissance, at this time in its full strength, when it thought consciously about the value of its more or less unconscious impulses, cast them aside in favor of its inherited traditions. In *Tamburlaine*, whose hero's interest was material, it regarded death as an end, but in *Faustus*, whose hero's interest was more than material, it still looked upon death as a beginning.

But even if, in Marlowe's time, the English Renaissance was not old enough to reflect in a new way about death, it is difficult, as I have already suggested, to overemphasize the importance of Marlowe's realization that, directly or indirectly, the fact of death raised problems that could be made the center of great drama. He had stated both the views which were possible to his contemporaries; without his lead, the later intensity about death might never have burnt through to expression, and Sir Philip Sidney's judgment on the incompetence of Elizabethan dramatists might have been the judgment of posterity.

2

As time wore on, the moral that had been somewhat naïvely expressed in *Tamburlaine* became more and more acutely felt; that aspect of death which made it the end of all things was more vividly realized, and the belief that lay behind *Faustus* became gradually more impotent and dim. Instead of fearing death as the beginning of eternal torment the Elizabethans feared it as the conclusion to all accomplishment. It was a kind of horrible joke which grinned at impotent desire and mocked all achievement into air. Because death destroyed them, beauty and power and wealth were hollow on their own account, not in comparison to the pleasures of heaven. "O eloquent, just, and mighty Death! . . . thou hast drawn together all the far-stretched greatness, all the pride, cruelty, and ambition of man, and covered it all over with these two narrow words, *Hic jacet*."

So, as the Renaissance advanced, it began to think more and more of death, and the drama began to express the conclusion at which, in Raleigh's words, it had arrived. It is perhaps merely a coincidence — though it is a very striking one — that this preoccupation with death begins at the moment when Queen Elizabeth was dying. In the last years of her life, the burst of passion about death which is Elizabethan tragedy was just beginning; not till after she had died did it reach its climax. She was in many ways the symbol of the Renaissance, of that respite of life before men began to realize once more the immense importance of death. When she became old, the Renaissance had also become old; when she died, it began to contemplate death. Elizabethan tragedy was the expression of this contemplation. It was far more concerned with death than any drama that had previously existed. Death, indeed, *was* tragedy; a tragedy was a play which ended in death. The Elizabethans did not think of a tragedy as " the imitation of an action . . . through pity and fear effecting the proper purgation of these emotions." [1] Nor was it

> . . . a certeyn storie . . .
> Of him that stood in greet prosperitee

---

1. Aristotle, *Poetics*, ch. vi, trans. Butcher.

> And is y-fallen out of heigh degree
> Into myserie, and endeth wretchedly. [2]

It was merely a story that ended in death:

> And tragical, my noble lord, it is;
> For Pyramus therein doth kill himself. [3]

There is thus more than merely biographical importance in the fact that Shakespeare stopped writing comedies in the first years of the seventeenth century. He simply expressed better than anyone else the trend of contemporary thought — a statement which is sufficiently proved by the popularity of his innovations, such as the graveyard scene. He began to contemplate life tragically, and like many of his contemporaries, and unlike Faustus, he began to express the new point of view which that contemplation aroused. Hamlet meditated on suicide a very few years before Donne wrote his treatise to prove that suicide was sometimes permissible. [4] And as we have seen, both of

2. Chaucer, *Monk's Prologue*, B 3163 ff.

3. *Midsummer Night's Dream*, v, 1. See Kyd, *Soliman and Perseda*, induction:

Death (to Love and Fortune):

> And I commaund you to forbeare this place;
> For heere the mouth of sad Melpomene
> Is wholy bent to tragedies discourse:
> *And what are Tragedies but acts of death?*

Also Fletcher's "Address to the Reader" prefaced to the first edition of *The Faithful Shepherdess*, where, speaking of a tragi-comedy, he says: "In respect it wants deaths . . . is enough to make it no tragedy."

4. I have drawn attention to further parallels between Hamlet's

them, though expressing new ideas, still clung to the old prohibitions. According to Donne, suicide was only to be allowed when God's glory would be advanced by it; Hamlet was stricter still, and held that the Almighty's canon forbade it entirely. Indeed Hamlet's reflections about life and death, as I have elsewhere remarked, are throughout profoundly significant of their time. Though it may be dangerous to draw too many inferences about a whole age from one expression in that age, we cannot, I think, go far wrong if we recognize Hamlet's voice, here and elsewhere, as the voice of the more thoughtful spirits among his contemporaries. It is the voice of a Renaissance grown middle-aged, when the confident bombast of a Tamburlaine is no longer possible. Spontaneity of action is gone; the world itself is less admirable than it once seemed:

I have of late, — but, wherefore, I know not, — lost all my mirth, foregone all custom of exercise; and indeed it goes so heavily with my disposition that this goodly frame, the earth, seems to me a sterile promontory; this most excellent canopy, the air, look you, this brave o'erhanging firmament, this majestical roof fretted with golden fire, why, it appears no other thing to me but a foul and pestilent congregation of vapors. What a piece of work is a man! How noble in reason! How infinite in faculty! In form and moving how express and admirable! In action how like an angel! In apprehension how

---

state of mind and Donne's in an article, "Donne and His Age," in *A Garland for John Donne*, Cambridge, Massachusetts, 1931, pp. 177 ff.

like a god! The beauty of the world! The paragon of animals!
And yet, to me, what is this quintessence of dust? man delights not me. . . .

It is not Hamlet alone who speaks, just as it is
not Hamlet alone who holds a skull. The English
Renaissance was becoming contemplative, and its
contemplation was led more and more, like Hamlet's, to death. But as it advanced, the less its
thoughts on the subject resembled those of the
Middle Ages. We already know how a fresh per-
ception, like an etcher's tool, can bite into an old
idea and produce something vivid and new. So, as
the spontaneity of the first period, when death was
not thought of at all, passed into the reflectiveness
of the early seventeenth century, those ideas which
we may attribute specifically to the Renaissance
became more and more clearly defined.

The well-known passage in *Measure for Measure*
is worth quoting once more:

Ay, but to die, and go we know not where;
To lie in cold obstruction and to rot;
This sensible warm motion to become
A kneaded clod; and the delighted spirit
To bathe in fiery floods, or to reside
In thrilling region of thick-ribbed ice;
To be imprison'd in the viewless winds,
And blown with restless violence round about
The pendant world; or to be worse than worst
Of those that lawless and incertain thoughts
Imagine howling: 'tis too horrible!
The weariest and most loathed worldly life

That age, ache, penury and imprisonment
Can lay on nature is a paradise
To what we fear of death.

The contrast to the last speech of Faustus is illuminating. What first occurs to Claudio's mind is the
destruction of the body, the decay of "sensible
warm motion"; after that, the fear of something
beyond death torments him. But, like Hamlet,
Claudio imagines far more generalized punish-
ments than Faustus. Faustus has a literal picture
of medieval hell before him; Claudio, though his
imagination is doubtless conditioned by the same
picture, goes beyond it into a vaster conception of
suffering. And his expressed conclusion is exactly
opposite to the implied conclusion of Faustus.
Claudio decides that no matter how bad this world
is, it is preferable to death; Faustus implies that no
matter how good this world is, a happy existence
in the next is far more valuable. The things of this
world are nothing to Faustus; the loss of them is
everything to Claudio. Claudio, however, still re-
gards the question of death from two sides: it is
not only an end to all happiness, it is the possible
beginning of torment. In the drama the Renaissance had yet to express with serious deliberation
its complete point of view.

In the great tragedies of Shakespeare this expression is not found so clearly as in the works
of some of his lesser contemporaries. *Othello*, *King*

Lear, *Macbeth*, as I have previously suggested, do not give us that peculiar Elizabethan flavor, that intense atmosphere of mortality, which we feel in the other dramatists who concentrated more upon death alone. The reason is plain enough, for Shakespeare stands head and shoulders above his contemporaries largely because of his ability to describe character; we are so aware of the living reality of his figures that their deaths are much less revealing than their lives. His tragedies are not tragedies because their heroes die; though death is their inevitable conclusion, its very inevitability makes it less significant. What matters is the personality of his people while they live; the way in which Shakespeare describes Lear, Othello, Hamlet, and Macbeth makes us think that death comes to them rather as a relief, painful and moving though it be, than as a catastrophe.

And yet without the contemporary conflict of ideas about death, it is doubtful whether such a profound contemplation of the essentials of human nature would have been possible. Shakespeare's depth of insight came as the result of that questioning of man's position in the world which the thousand complicated tendencies of the Renaissance, all tending to be focussed on the fact of death, had evolved. But though his use of the conventions of death is invariably illuminating, and his characters contemplate death with passion and from many points of view, he is less revealing for our present purpose than his contemporaries. He does not study death for its own sake, like Tourneur, Chapman, Webster, and Ford. To these dramatists, as being more representative, we must now turn.

3

We have already noticed the famous scene in Tourneur's *Revenger's Tragedy* (III, 4) where Vendice presents the skull of his beloved to the lecherous Duke. Vendice's speech, as he contemplates the horrible contrivance, is worth quoting at length:

And now methinks I could e'en chide myself
For doting on her beauty, though her death
Shall be revenged after no common action.
Does the silkworm expend her yellow labors
For thee? For thee does she undo herself?
Are lordships sold to maintain ladyships,
For the poor benefit of a bewitching minute?
Why does yon fellow falsify highways,
And put his life between the judge's lips,
To refine such a thing — keeps horse and men
To beat their valors for her?
Surely we are all mad people, and they
Whom we think are, are not. . . .
Does every proud and self-affecting dame
Camphire her face for this, and grieve her Maker
In sinful baths of milk, when many an infant starves
For her superfluous outside — all for this?
Who now bids twenty pounds a night? prepares
Music, perfumes, and sweetmeats? All are hushed.
Thou may'st lie chaste now! it were fine, methinks,

> To have thee seen at revels, forgetful feasts
> And unclean brothels! sure, 'twould fright the sinner,
> And make him a good coward: put a reveller
> Out of his antic amble,
> And cloy an epicure with empty dishes.

The whole speech is exceptionally interesting, apart from its superb poetry, for it expresses a development of feeling beyond that in Marlowe and *Measure for Measure*. There are, as so often in the Elizabethan period, two strands which go to make up this feeling. The first is typically Renaissance; Marlowe had expressed it in *Tamburlaine*: death is the destructive end of all things. But there is a profound difference between Tourneur's expression and Marlowe's. To Tamburlaine death was unexpected; when it came it was unprepared for. But here there is no question of the death of an individual; the subject itself is reflected on apart from any of its actual consequences on the stage, and as far as the surface plot is concerned, the reflection seems at first entirely gratuitous. That it is not gratuitous, however, becomes clear on a moment's consideration. In fact the contrary is true, for Vendice's remarks are, as other critics have observed, really the theme of the play. Without them it would lose almost a whole dimension. To have the specific action bound together and intensified by an impassioned series of generalizations about the implications of that action gives it a new kind of universality.

But here, as in Claudio's speech on death, there is something else beside the general deliberation on death's finality. Claudio thought of the next world, Vendice thinks of the emptiness of this. The contemplation of death has still a moral significance; and the moral is the old one of earth's vanity. To think of death is to forsake sin, to leave "forgetful feasts and unclean brothels," to cease to grieve one's Maker by sinful baths of milk. But just as the first strand of feeling is far removed from its earlier expression in Tamburlaine, so is this second and more moral strand far different from what it would have been in the Middle Ages. The death's head is applied as an afterthought. What first occurs to Vendice is the passing of earthly things; only at the end of his reflections is the other position taken, and though, like Skelton, when his "honorable jentylwoman" sent him the "ugly tokyn," Vendice comes to the conclusion that man is but dust, nevertheless he does not turn for refuge to the other world. On the contrary, his beloved's death "shall be revenged after no common action."

Tourneur represents, then, a further aspect of Elizabethan expression, and his moments of best writing are when he considers death. Death concerns him, in spite of the moral alloy in his reflections, chiefly in that it brings life to an end. Life matters above all things:

1st noble:　　　　　　　　And for natural death,
　　　　　　I hope it will be threescore years acoming.
Lussurioso: True? no more but threescore years?
1st noble: Fourscore, I hope, my lord.
2nd noble: And fivescore, I.
3rd noble: But 'tis my hope, my lord, you shall ne'er die.
Lussurioso: Give me thy hand; these others I rebuke . . .
　　　　　　Thou shalt sit next me.

(Revenger's Tragedy, v, 3)

So the hero of *The Atheist's Tragedy*, D'Amville, is most real in those moments when the fear of death surges upon him (v, 2):

> But infuse
> A little poison in a potion when
> Thou giv'st me physic, unawares to me.
> So shall I steal into my grave without
> The understanding or the fear of death.
> And that's the end I aim at. For the thought
> Of death is a most fearful torment; is it not?

These are not medieval sentiments. If the thought of death is a torment because of what comes after it, then to die suddenly like this, as Montaigne wished to die, is the worst of all possible deaths. On the other hand, it is the best if death be considered a conclusion rather than a beginning.

4

The Revenger's Tragedy was published in 1607; *The Atheist's Tragedy* probably appeared soon after or before. At just about the same time three great plays were being written, which, more than any others, sum up Elizabethan thought about death. These are the Bussy and Byron plays of Chapman; in them we have a discussion of human life in terms of neo-Stoic philosophy, and consequently a study of death as the climax to that life. It is significant of the time that this discussion, like the debate in *Faustus*, took place on the stage, for it shows once more how the deepest elements of Elizabethan thought found their most significant expression in popular literature, and it shows how the dramatists were working toward a wider dramatic form, in which thought and action, reflection and passion, should be part of the same artistic whole. Chapman, like Shakespeare, was not a disciple of Marlowe for nothing.

Many writers have observed that the Renaissance marked the escape of the individual from the bonds of authority; and the statement may be accepted, in part at least, as true; for an attempt to escape — if not the escape itself — was certainly made. Man viewing himself in new relations naturally desired to shake off the limitations of the old; he desired, in other words, to be independent. And this desire is the key to Chapman. To him man's wish to be "self-made" is the chief aim of existence, and Chapman proceeds to work out the problems which this aim produces in the three most interesting, if not the greatest, of his plays.

It is necessary to study them in their chronological order: first, *Bussy D'Ambois* (printed 1607), second, *The Conspiracy and Tragedy of Charles, Duke of Byron* (printed 1608), and third, *The Revenge of Bussy D'Ambois* (printed 1613, probably written two or three years earlier). Each play takes for its hero a man who desires to make himself independent of external circumstances. Life, for Chapman, is a struggle between the individual and "Nature" (here he is original and modern in using this term instead of Destiny or Fortune) — a tragedy which ends in defeat for the former because he cannot control himself. He cannot *make* himself what he wants to be, or, granted his potentialities, what he should be. He is continually giving false emphasis to worldly things; he continually acts from a wrong sense of values.

The tragedy of Bussy is just this; he is swayed by desires over which he has no control. In the first place he succumbs to his environment by seeking advancement at court (which to Chapman, who was elaborating a contemporary convention, was the symbol of hollowness), and in the second place he falls a victim to sensual passion. These weaknesses are his undoing, and though, with false security, he has considered himself self-sufficient ("who to himself is law, no law doth need"), he falls on account of them. He is proud and confident, but he dies because of these tragic flaws.

> Is my body, then,
> But penetrable flesh? And must my mind
> Follow my blood? Can my divine part add
> No aid to th'earthly in extremity?
> Then these divines are but for forms, not fact . . .
> . . . let my death,
> Define life nothing but a courtier's breath.

And again, just before he dies:

> O frail condition of strength, valor, virtue,
> In me (like warning fire upon the top
> Of some steep beacon, on a steeper hill)
> Made to express it: like a falling star
> Silently glanc'd, that like a thunderbolt
> Look'd to have stuck and shook the firmament.

There is here much that reminds us of the plays we have already examined. Bussy, like Tamburlaine, is a typical Renaissance hero; it is a decided shock to him to realize that his body is "but penetrable flesh." Immersed in a life of action, death had appeared to him, as it had appeared to Tamburlaine, a possibility so remote that it was almost incredible when it finally arrived. But Bussy's response is different from Tamburlaine's. He does not gloat over his previous conquests; life itself, since it comes so suddenly to an end, is worth only "a courtier's breath." Nor does this fact, as in Tourneur, produce moralizings; it is sufficiently tragic in itself. Bussy's career has been abortive, he has accomplished only a few days' glory; there has been no explosion to make his name famous in the world.

It is because death brings his career to an end that life is worthless; for death reveals to both the audience and himself the weaknesses that have made life empty.

In the Byron plays, the problem is attacked from another angle. Here there are no women to distract or weaken; the catastrophe is produced from something else — from false security. Byron believes that he *has* control over himself, that he *is* self-made and self-sufficient. He is "glorious," to use Chapman's description of him. Consequently he is destroyed by his own pride. He has gone too far; he has not, in Clermont D'Ambois' words, given

> glad obedience
> To anything the high and general Cause
> To match with his whole fabric, hath ordain'd;
> > (*Revenge*, IV, I)

he is more self-sufficient than the facts of life justify.

As a result his death is a long and violent protest. The fifth act of *Byron's Tragedy* contains some of the finest poetry in English, and is the most complete presentation of a reaction to death in all Elizabethan drama.

Byron has been manipulating a conspiracy against Henry IV. The conspiracy is discovered, and Byron refuses to ask the King's pardon, though the King is willing to grant it. Consequently Byron is tried for treason, and is condemned to be executed.

Byron makes his first significant speech about death when he is talking to his friends while waiting for the decision of his judges:

> Is't possible the King should be so vain
> To think he can shake me with fear of death?
> Or make me apprehend that he intends it?
> Thinks he to make his firmest men his clouds?
>
> (v, 3)

We are assured by Byron himself that he is impervious to the fear of death. But this is exactly what he is not. He sees the judges entering, and guesses the truth at once:

> O then I am but dead,
> Now, now ye come all to pronounce my sentence.
> I am condemn'd unjustly. . . .
> You have not done
> Like a good Justice, and one that knew
> He sat upon the precious blood of virtue;
> Y'ave pleas'd the cruel King.

He continues in this vein, attacking the judges, for some time, with passionate declarations of his own innocence and their corruption. He next begs the King, almost furiously, for pardon, and gives a eulogy of his own virtues as savior of his country. This calls forth the following comment from the Chancellor:

> I fear his frenzy; never saw I man
> Of such a spirit so amaz'd at death.

He is brought to the scaffold; and a bishop approaches him with an appeal for his soul. Byron's reply is striking:

> Horror of death! Let me alone in peace.
> And leave my soul to me, whom it concerns;
> You have no charge of it.

And in a long and magnificent speech he proceeds to declare that he knows already what the bishop will tell him — that the body is but a "sink of folly," "a slave bound face to face to Death,"

> And what said all you more? I know, besides,
> That life is but a dark and stormy night
> Of senseless dreams, terrors, and broken sleeps;
> A tyranny, devising pains to plague
> And make man long in dying, racks his death;
> And Death is nothing; what can you say more?
> I being a large globe, and a little earth,
> Am seated like the earth, betwixt both the heavens,
> That if I rise, to heaven I rise; if fall,
> I likewise fall to heaven; what stronger faith
> Hath any of your souls? What say you more?
> Why lose I time in these things?   Talk of knowledge!
> It serves for inward use. I will not die
> Like to a clergyman; but like the captain
> That pray'd on horseback, and with sword in hand,
> Threaten'd the sun, commanding it to stand.

Byron, that is, is fully aware of all the old platitudes, but will have none of them; he stands alone. And finally, after protesting against the reading of his sentence, threatening his executioner, and frantically asking if a pardon has arrived, he pulls himself together, as the convention of a hero's brave death almost forced him to do, and he dies nobly, with the utterance of the best poetry Chapman ever wrote:

> And so farewell for ever! Never more
> Shall any hope of my revival see me;
> Such is the endless exile of dead men.
> Summer succeeds the Spring; Autumn the Summer;
> The frosts of Winter the fall'n leaves of Autumn:
> All these and all fruits in them yearly fade,
> And every year return: but cursed man
> Shall never more renew his vanish'd face. . . .
> Strike, strike, O strike; fly, fly, commanding soul,
> And on thy wings for this thy body's breath,
> Bear the eternal victory of Death! [5]

With this act before us, we may say that we have at last the Renaissance opinion completely expressed. Death is not, as in Tamburlaine, an unforeseen event cutting off a spontaneous, almost childlike life; it is not, as in Faustus, the beginning of eternal torment. It is complete finality. Byron does not think, like Claudio, of future punishment,

5. The reader is likely to be somewhat confused at the sudden change, on Byron's part, from fear of death to a brave acceptance of it, and doubtless Chapman, like Marlowe when describing the death of Tamburlaine, could have handled the situation better than he did. The change, however, had to be made, for the convention that a hero must die nobly was too strong to be violated even by such an innovator and lover of paradox as Chapman. On the stage the change is not so noticeable. At a performance of *The Conspiracy and Tragedy of Byron* given in London by the Elizabethan Stage Circle in the summer of 1929 (the only performance of this play since the first half of the seventeenth century), the final speeches of Byron seemed, in the mouth of a competent actor, very true and moving, and no inconsistency appeared.

and he definitely dismisses the old medieval moralizing, traces of which we still found in Tourneur. He will not accept death as a proof of life's vanity and emptiness; he will take it as the active end of an active existence; he will die like a soldier, fighting. It is this deliberate repudiation of the medieval teaching which makes Byron's death so different from Tamburlaine's. In that first enthusiasm of which *Tamburlaine* was the expression, such ideas were not thought of at all; here they are thought of, and are consciously spurned. In every detail, the opposition to the Middle Ages is shown. Consider Byron's use of the word *exile* — "the endless exile of dead men." The Middle Ages spoke of man's *life* as an exile, but here his exile is death; the application of the word is completely reversed, and the reversal shows more plainly than anything else how Byron as a symbol of the Renaissance emphasized the present world instead of the world to come.

In this sense, the contrast between Byron's death and the death of Faustus is particularly illuminating. For Byron thinks of the next world with assurance; he is certain of heaven, and the thought of hell does not enter his mind. He has no sense of sin, and he scorns the priests who offer him comfort.[6]

6. In this detail Chapman is in direct opposition to his source: Edward Grimeston's *General Inventorie of the History of France*, London, 1607, p. 991. See T. M. Parrott's edition of Chapman's

He has considered himself capable of everything; it is for this reason that death is such a terrible revelation. The forces he had neglected destroy him, and death is his disillusioning end.

So much, then, for this aspect of man's problems. In *Bussy* Chapman had decided that the emphasis on false values was destructive because it loosened self-control; in *Byron* he had come to the conclusion that man must not too easily think himself self-sufficient, for death will destroy him. The solution was yet to come.

In the *Revenge of Bussy D'Ambois*, the last play of the series, it is presented. Clermont D'Ambois, Bussy's brother (who, it may be noted, is entirely Chapman's invention), is the only one of Chapman's chief characters who has kept the right proportion. How he did this we already know from our discussion of him at the end of Chapter IV. He had solved the dualism of life, had joined "himself with the Universe,"

> Not plucking from the whole his wretched part
> And into straits, or into nought revert,
> Wishing the complete Universe might be
> Subject to such a rag of it as he;
>
> (IV, 1)

Tragedies, London, 1910, pp. 622–623. On the whole, however, Chapman follows Grimeston's account fairly closely. Byron's death as there told is itself singularly moving and typical of the Renaissance, even without Chapman's more reflective additions.

he was scornful of "riches and greatness," of "all things servile and ignoble"; he had none of the faults of Bussy or Byron. And at the end he committed suicide. He did it, not because of any overwhelming disaster, but merely because his purpose in life was accomplished, and he had nothing left to live for. He died as he had lived, independent of opinion, "fix'd in himself."

And here the expression of new opinion in the drama, as might have been inferred from our previous discussion, reaches the most interesting point of its career. It mounts to a climax, and at that climax is defeated. Byron, whose protest against death and the platitudes of the Middle Ages is so typical of the time, comes to an imperfect end because of the defects which are inherent in his egotistical point of view. Clermont *is* the perfect individual, but in being so he relapses into the defeatist position his generation had done its best to grow away from. He is independent, but he buys his independence at the cost of vitality. There is nothing in Clermont of that fine exuberance about life which we find in Tamburlaine and in Byron. He is resigned to all that a difficult life can bring, he accomplishes his purpose with a kind of melancholy abstraction.[7] Chapman built him out of

7. Clermont has been, with justice, compared to Hamlet in this respect. See T. M. Parrott's introduction to the play in his edition of Chapman's *Tragedies*.

Stoic principles, and Stoic principles are the reverse of enthusiastic. By this return to Stoicism we may say that the Renaissance, as far as it was expressed in the drama, was defeated. Chapman, there can be little doubt, was the most "thoughtful" of all the Elizabethan dramatists; his being so makes his Stoicism all the more significant. For Stoicism had originally expressed more fully than anything except Christianity the gradual dying out of the feeling for the beauty and value of earthly life. It was the expression of the human spirit grown old and tired; like much of the orthodox teaching of the late Middle Ages, it was entirely disillusioned. And disillusioned is the word which best fits Clermont D'Ambois. His individualism is the pale individualism of a fatalist: he does not protest, he submits. He has none of his brother's energy; to him the world is without value, and when one's work is done, one should escape from life by one's own hand.

In this Stoic fashion the Elizabethan emphasis on death was most fully expressed. Almost as soon as the age had given voice to the new point of view, it returned — in a different way — to the old. The license given to suicide was original and fresh, but the cause for suicide was the same cause which all through the fourteenth, fifteenth, and sixteenth centuries had made death the chief object of contemplation: the emptiness of life. Chapman, in his treatment of death, was, in spite of his originality, a reactionary. He turned to those elements of classicism which were most medieval to express the emotions which the Renaissance had finally aroused. Hence, in spite of his conscious learning, he too, like his contemporaries, combined the two elements which were the background of his time. He is classical in his interest in a successful worldly life; he is medieval in his emphasis on the manner of death as the most significant fact of existence.

5

John Webster was the last of the dramatists to study death with fervor and passion. He was one of the natural successors to Chapman; his two great tragedies are full of a dark yet fiery pessimism which is complementary to the more intellectual melancholy of his predecessor. Webster's heroes and heroines are whirled rapidly through a life that is doomed, one feels, from the moment it is first set in action. In *The White Devil* and *The Duchess of Malfi* we are in a black and oppressive atmosphere where death is a matter of poisoned helmets, of coffins, of madness and horror. It is, to some extent, the atmosphere of Tourneur, but there is one profound difference. In Tourneur life was worth prolonging, and death was its objectionable end. Death, too, still called forth moralizings, in the old-fashioned way, about life. But in Webster's tragedies there is no need to moralize: the action itself proves life bitter and unreasoning. Once one is used to Webster's atmosphere, it no longer seems a dramatic flaw that Ferdinand's destruction of the Duchess of Malfi is insufficiently motivated; the very unreasonableness of his antagonism makes it a more accurate reflection of the irrational antagonism of life itself. For life, in Webster's tragedies, is almost as horrible as death:

> Of what is't fools make such vain keeping?
> Sin their conception, their birth weeping,
> Their life a general mist of error,
> Their death a hideous storm of terror.
>
> (*Duchess of Malfi*, IV, 2)

And the Duchess, just before she dies, says (IV, 2):

> Tell my brothers
> That I perceive death, now I am well awake,
> Best gift is they can give or I can take.

Death is, indeed, the only solution for Webster's persecuted and unhappy heroines. The almost insane desire with which Ferdinand and Ludovico and the rest seek to destroy them must be satisfied; in death these unhappy women escape the torment their lives have been made;

> We cease to grieve, cease to be fortune's slaves,
> Nay, cease to die, by dying.
>
> (*White Devil*, V, 6)

Death is horrible chiefly because it occurs in horrible circumstances — in the midst of madmen, in the torture of poisoning; not because the fact itself is appalling. Consequently Webster's heroines die bravely. Their lives have been terrible enough, "death doth not fright" them. Death does not appall even the villains. Flamineo (*White Devil*, v, 6) says,

> I do not look
> Who went before, nor who shall follow me;
> No, at myself I will begin and end. . . .
> 'Tis well there's yet some goodness in my death;
> My life was a black charnel. I have caught
> An everlasting cold; I have lost my voice
> Most irrecoverably.

Bosola dies with the same sort of resigned pessimism (*Duchess of Malfi*, v, 5):

> O, this gloomy world!
> In what a shadow, or deep pit of darkness,
> Doth womanish and fearful mankind live!
> Let worthy minds ne'er stagger in distrust
> To suffer death or shame for what is just;
> Mine is another voyage.

To Webster it is indeed a gloomy world. Life is overshadowed by death, a death which is universal and inevitable, but which is also somewhat of a relief, for at least it brings the sadistic cruelty of the external world to an end. And if the external world is relentless in its will to inflict death, even the individual, of whose prowess the Renaissance had at first so confidently boasted, is no refuge to himself:

> I am i' the way to study a long silence:
> To prate were idle. I remember nothing.

> There's nothing of so infinite vexation
> As man's own thoughts.
>
> (*White Devil*, v, 6)

6

Ford's treatment of death represents the end of Elizabethan drama. He may often say the same things as Fletcher, but he is poetically more interesting, and historically he is more revealing than Middleton, Massinger, or Shirley. What first strikes us, in reading him, is that all feeling of protest against the fact of death has disappeared. He too, in a different way from that of Webster, is a logical follower of Chapman. Death is always soothing to his characters; they express no resentment or bitterness at the world they are so ready to leave. Eroclea, in *The Lover's Melancholy* (iv, 3), speaks in a manner very characteristic of Ford:

> Minutes are number'd by the fall of sands,
> As by an hourglass; the span of time
> Doth waste us to our graves, and we look on it:
> An age of pleasures, revell'd out, comes home
> At last, and ends in sorrow; but the life,
> Weary of riot, numbers every sand,
> Wailing in sighs, until the last drop down;
> So to conclude calamity in rest.

Similar remarks can be found throughout Ford's plays; they may appear in the mouths of any of the serious characters. A resigned acceptance of inevitable doom haunts them all; time and fate hang heavily upon them:

Brother, dear brother, know what I have been,
And know that now there's but a dining-time
'Twixt us and our confusion,

cries Annabella (*'Tis Pity*, v, 5). The same sense of
fatality that hovers over this play is expressed by
Penthea in *The Broken Heart* (ii, 3):

Penthea: In vain we labor in this course of life
To piece our journey out at length, or crave
Respite of breath; our home is in the grave.
Bassanes: Perfect philosophy!

This prevailing tone, combined with Ford's characteristic desire to make the most of highly emotional situations, accounts for the fact that he,
more consistently than almost any other Elizabethan
dramatist, plays up the death of his heroes and
heroines. A brave facing of death, as we already
know, was one of the essentials for a "good" Elizabethan character; Ford relies on the convention
continually. Perkin Warbeck's remarks are typical:

Death? pish! 'tis but a sound; a name of air;
A minute's storm, or not so much; to tumble
From bed to bed, be massacred alive
By some physicians, for a month or two,
In hope of freedom from a fever's torments,
Might stagger manhood; here the pain is past
Ere sensibly 'tis felt. Be men of spirit!
Spurn coward passion! so illustrious mention
Shall blaze our names, and stile us Kings o'er death.

(v, 3)

The characters in *The Broken Heart* seem always

aware of their approaching dissolution; the King knows he is soon to die, Ithocles speaks of it:

> Death waits to waft me to the Stygian banks,
> And free me from this chaos of my bondage;
>
> (III, 2)

Penthea's speeches are full of death longing:

> My glass of life, sweet princess, hath few minutes
> Remaining to run down; the sands are spent;
> For by an inward messenger I feel
> The summons of departure short and certain.
>
> (III, 5)

And when the actual moment of death comes, these characters welcome it with a kind of rapture. At such moments Ford produces a new and, in the drama, final emotion about death, for though the style may be very handsome, the emotion is of decaying or decayed vitality. We have only to keep Tamburlaine in mind when reading the following speech to realize how much dramatic emotion had changed. Ithocles is speaking; these are his last words:

> Thoughts of ambition, or delicious banquet
> With beauty, youth, and love, together perish
> In my last breath, which on the sacred altar
> Of a long looked for peace — now — moves — to heaven.
>
> (IV, 4)

The famous death of Calantha in this play is the most striking of Ford's death scenes. First we are shown an altar, then the body of Ithocles is carried in, richly crowned; Calantha makes a kind of testament and puts a wedding ring on the finger of the dead Ithocles:

> Thus I new-marry him, whose wife I am;
> Death shall not separate us. Oh, my lords,
> I but deceived your eyes with antic gesture,
> When one news straight came huddling on another,
> Of death! and death! and death! still I danced forward,
> But it struck home, and here, and in an instant.
> Be such mere women, who, with shrieks and outcries,
> Can vow a present end to all their sorrows,
> Yet live to court new pleasures, and out live them:
> They are the silent griefs which cut the heart strings.[8]

She kisses the lips of Ithocles, and orders the song to be sung which she had "fitted" for her end:

> Glories, pleasures, pomps, delights and ease
>   Can but please
> The outward senses when the mind
> Is or untroubled, or by peace refined.
> Crowns may flourish and decay,
> Beauties shine, but fade away.
> Youth may revel, yet it must
> Lie down in a bed of dust.
> Earthly honors flow and waste,
> Time alone doth change and last.
> Sorrows mingled with contents, prepare
>   Rest for care;
> Love only reigns in death. . . .

It is hard to see how the dramatic treatment of death could be carried further than this without

---

8. There is no more successful version than this of the old Senecan tag, probably the commonest of all such in the Elizabethan drama: "Curae leves loquuntur, ingentes stupent," *Hippolytus*, 615.

falling into the emotional opportunism of Fletcher and Shirley. Ford, in spite of his decadent characteristics,[9] has still enough artistic integrity to produce that unity of tone which is a necessary part of dramatic and poetic illusion. And yet there is a great difference between his way of writing and that of Webster or Tourneur. The following speech from his *Lover's Melancholy* (II, 2) is on exactly the same subject as Vendice's address to the skull in *The Revenger's Tragedy* (above, p. 238), but it is treated in quite a different way. The style is excellent, the repetitions — repetition is one of Ford's favorite and most successful stylistic devices — are cleverly handled, but the thought is not seized by the poet's mind with that immediacy and vigor which characterize Tourneur. Tourneur's ethical intensity, like Webster's bitterness, is missing; the truth is described as a general truth, unrelated to moral indignation or moral value; the imagery is also more generalized, less tautly conceived:

> fools, desperate fools!
> You are cheated, grossly cheated; range on, range on,
> And roll about the world to gather moss,
> The moss of honor, gay reports, gay clothes,
> Gay wives, huge empty buildings, whose proud roofs
> Shall with their pinnacles even reach the stars!

---

9. These have been well discussed by S. P. Sherman, "Ford's Contribution to the Decadence of the Drama," in Bang's *Materialien zur Kunde des älteren Englischen Dramas*, vol. 23, Leipzig, 1908, by T. S. Eliot, *Selected Essays* ("John Ford"), by Miss Bradbrook, *op. cit.*

Ye work and work like blind moles in the paths
That are bored through the crannies of the earth,
To charge your hungry souls with such full surfeits,
As, being gorg'd once, make you lean with plenty;
And when you have skimm'd the vomit of your riots,
You are fat in no felicity but folly:
Then your last sleeps seize on you; then the troops
Of worms crawl round, and feast, good cheer, rich fare,
Dainty, delicious!

It is significant that Tourneur's speech is an essential part of the structure of his play, whereas Ford's is relatively incidental; the reflection is used for ornament, it does not bind the play together. There is a close connection between this technical irresponsibility and that emphasis on emotion for its own sake, so characteristic of all Ford's writing, which has been described as moral anarchy.

7

After Ford there is no dramatist whose treatment of death is of real interest. There is no passionate realization of death, no violent emotion concerning it. The high seriousness of the great period, when popular literature, for so brief a time, had vividly described the most important feelings about death, was over. With Fletcher the stage became the home of those romantic evasions which it for so long afterwards had to endure, and popular literature was once more entertainment, rather than catharsis. Death was made much of, but nothing

new was said about it. Fletcher repeated what
countless numbers of people had repeated before
him; he was content with the externals of life, and
he observed only the externals of death. The subject had perhaps been exhausted; at any rate the
period of strong emotion had come to an end.

But if we cast our eyes back over the period as a
whole, we find that much has happened since the
Elizabethan drama began. Marlowe, as we observed, was the first to use the stage as the vehicle
for serious presentation of high things, and in so
using it he was the first of the Elizabethans to make
death dramatic. Not only is his treatment of death
the earliest fully dramatic treatment, but his attitude toward the subject is the most typically Elizabethan. In *Tamburlaine*, death is the end of life; in
Faustus, it is the beginning of torment. And in a
sense the subsequent dramatic treatment of death
is a development of these two ideas. The first became more and more emphasized; the second was
pushed more and more out of the way. The Elizabethan dramatists tried, it would seem, to realize as
completely as possible that aspect of death which
Tamburlaine had expressed without much thought;
they (or rather their characters) felt with increasing
sincerity that death is the end of worldly things.
Claudio expressed this attitude, still mixed with
medieval reminiscences; Tourneur's Vendice did
the same thing, though the reminiscences are of

another category. Only in Chapman, in *Byron's Tragedy*, was this aspect of death realized at the same time passionately and without any remnants of medieval opinion. Byron is a more thoughtful Tamburlaine — more mature in that he recognizes the implications of life's futility that death makes evident — and entirely of the Renaissance in spurning those implications as of no value.

But this victory of the Renaissance point of view was only momentary; in *Byron's Tragedy* itself one feels that Chapman disapproved of his hero's attitude; in the following play he definitely expressed that disapproval by setting up as a model a character of an entirely different type, who in his disillusionment is a reversion to the more medieval point of view. And after Chapman, life, when passionately described on the stage, is no longer admirable at all; it is, on the contrary, "a general mist of error," and the fragment of man's nobility that life leaves shining, gleams brightly only in death.

Yet Elizabethan tragedy, by its contemplation of death, altered the previous conception of it enormously. For Webster's gloom about life is not the medieval gloom, it does not make heaven shine more happily by contrast. It is an unbiased and realistic picture, the product of a dark nature, itself the product of the darkening Renaissance, not of an inherited belief. The return to the older point of view, in Webster, is by no means complete; death is still chiefly an end, even if only an end to something horrible rather than to something fine. And Ford's paganism, his emphasis on emotion by itself without reference to a moral standard, seem, as one looks back over the whole period, the almost inevitable conclusion to the development I have tried to indicate. All his chief characters have the same attitude to death: they welcome it — even the most active of them — languorously, with a kind of tired voluptuousness. They do not reflect upon their past lives with pleasure, they do not praise the world they are so willing to leave; there is only acceptance and resignation. In his treatment of death, as in his handling of all emotional subjects, Ford is the last of the great Elizabethans.

8

But since the medieval emphasis on death was the background against which the drama grew, and may be considered one of the elements of its greatness, when the drama faded this background, which after all had never been forgotten, still remained. For a time it even seemed predominant, as it had been before, and there were many indications that its teachings were as vigorously urged as ever. Hence, in order to round out our study, we must end by leaving the drama behind.

There is no one, for our purpose, more significant than John Donne. One of his early prose works, the *Biathanatos*, was, as we know, somewhat heretical; but after his ordination heresy was the last thing he could be accused of. Donne, like his medieval predecessors, and like Webster,

> was much possessed by death,
> And saw the skull beneath the skin.

He too was "expert beyond experience" in the contemplation of another world:

All mankind is of one author, and is one volume; when one man dies, one chapter is not torn out of the book, but translated into a better language; and every chapter must be so translated: God employs several translators; some pieces are translated by age, some by sickness, some by war, some by justice; but God's hand is in every translation, and his hand shall bind up all our scattered leaves again, for that library where every book shall lie open to one another.[10]

No wonder death translates to a better language, for man in the flesh is wretched:

I would not make man worse than he is, nor his condition more miserable than it is. But could I though I would? As a man cannot flatter God, nor overpraise him, so a man cannot injure man, nor undervalue him.[11]

This whole world is but an universal church-yard, but our common grave, and the life and motion that the greatest persons have in it is but as the shaking of buried bodies in their grave, by an earthquake.[12] That which we call life is but *hebdomada mortium*, a week of death, seven days, seven periods

---

10. Donne, *Devotions* (1624), Meditation XVII.
11. *Ibid.*, Meditation XIV.
12. See Webster, *Duchess of Malfi*, v, 4 (Antonio's dying speech):
    "Pleasure of life, what is't? only the good hours
    Of an ague."

of our life spent in dying, a dying seven times over; and there is an end. Our birth dies in infancy, and our infancy dies in youth, and youth and the rest die in age, and age also dies and determines all. Nor do all these, youth out of infancy, or age out of youth, arise so, as the phoenix out of the ashes of another phoenix formerly dead, but as an asp or a serpent out of a carrion, or as a snake out of dung. . . . How much worse a death than death is this life, which so good men would so often change for death! [13]

This is all familiar. It is the old cry of the late Middle Ages; its teaching is the teaching that Petrarch put into the mouth of St. Augustine. Death consumes everything; we must look for the life beyond the grave, for the grave makes man nothing. The king and the private man must

in the dust of the grave be published, and (such are the revolutions of the grave) be mingled with the dust of every highway and of every dunghill, and swallowed in every puddle and pond. This is the most inglorious and contemptible vilification, the most deadly and peremptory nullification of man, that we can consider. [14]

Hamlet, too, had thought of how "a king may go a progress through the guts of a beggar," but he had done so to express his own revulsion, not to humble man's pride. It is that which is so significant in Donne. He completes the circle, and once more thinks passionately of death as the beginning of true life. [15]

13. "Death's Duel" (Donne's last sermon), printed in *Devotions*, London, 1840, pp. 209–210.

14. *Ibid.*, p. 215.

15. There are, of course, many expressions about death in Donne

The rebirth of the old attitude is often expressed in the early seventeenth century. William Loe, to mention an obscure religious writer, says in the epistle dedicatory to his *Songs of Sion* (1620):

O then let us meditate and muse to our selves, and sing and say to our selves, that our end and the last things, are not the least but the best things that we can consider of to mortifie us and make us meete for the saving mercies of God in Christ.[16]

Even Drummond of Hawthornden, who was not an ecclesiastic, preaches the same moral. Indeed, his "Cypresse Grove" (1623) is of the greatest interest, for it shows the Renaissance mind in process of ebbing back to the medieval level. Drummond begins by contemplating death as an end; it is

the sade Estranger of acquantance, the eternall Divorcer of Mariage, the Ravisher of the Children from their Parents . . . the Interrer of Fame,[17] the sole cause of Forgetfulnesse, by which the living talke of those gone away as of so manie Shadowes, or fabulous Paladines.[18]

---

that are not medieval. For instance, "Our critical day is not he very day of our death, but the whole course of our life." "Death's Duel," p. 218. And in his *Devotions*, the emphasis on death is a more personal matter than it was in the Middle Ages; a natural consequence, perhaps, of Protestantism. But these are only minor differences.

16. Ed. A. B. Grosart, *Miscellanies of the Fuller Worthies' Library*, London, 1871, I, 487.

17. This is the exact opposite of what Petrarch said; according to him, Fame triumphed over Death (*Triumph of Fame*).

18. Drummond, *Poetical Works*, ed. L. E. Kastner, Manchester, 1913, II, 69. The sources for this work are Montaigne, I, 19, and II, 12, Pierre Charron, *De la Sagesse*, and Innocenzio Ringhieri,

But he soon goes on to another point of view. Is death so horrible after all? "Is this life so great a good that the lose of it should bee so deare unto Man?" The answer, of course, is "No." Life is nothing; it may be destroyed by a

reflexe of the Sunne, a blast of winde. . . . And who would not rather than remaine chained in this loathsome Galley of the World, Sleepe ever (that is dye) having all thinges at one stay, bee free from those Vexationes, Disasteres, Contempts, Indignities, and manie manie Anguishes, unto which this Life is envassalled and made thrall?

Joys are only sorrows disguised: "O! who if before hee had a beeing, hee could have knowledge of the manie-fold Miseries of it, would enter this woefull Hospitall of the World, and accept of life upon such hard conditiones?" Death is really nothing; pure souls desire to die young.[19] Ambition for Fame? It is fatuous. Monuments are soon razed; literary renown soon dies; desert and virtue are rarely celebrated: "Dayes, Monthes, and Yeares, are

---

Dialoghi della vita et della morte, Bologna, 1550. This latter work I have not been able to consult; but it is interesting to observe that Drummond should go back for part of his material to a period before the change of attitude about death had occurred.

19. "To dye young is to doe that soone, and in some fewer dayes, which once thou must doe; it is but *the giving over of a Game that* (after never so manye hazardes) *must be lost*" (p. 85). This sounds like a reminiscence of Beaumont and Fletcher, *Philaster*, III, 1. Bellario (of death):

> I know, besides,
> It is but *giving over of a game*
> *That must be lost.*

swallowed up in the great Gulfe of Tyme (which puts out the eyes of all their Glorie) and onelie a fattall oblivion remaines." Death releases us from prison, frees us from an "infected and leprous Inne"; it is only a "short, nay, sweete sigh; and is not worthie the remembrance, compared with the smallest dram of the infinite Felicitie" of heaven. "Thinke then by Death, that thy Shell is broken, and thou then but even hatched; that thou art a Pearle, raised from thy Mother, to bee enchaced in Gold, and that the death-day of thy bodie, is thy birth-day to Eternitie." The work, like Cyprian's *De Mortalitate*, ends with a radiant vision of bliss.

One can see how the new point of view which the drama had expressed was apparently lost. To Drummond, to Donne, to William Loe (and they are only three out of countless similar writers), the world is nothing, man is nothing, fame is nothing. Death is the beginning of felicity. The passion about death which had shaken the drama caught religion once more, and, with its religious connotations, exhibited the same symptoms it had exhibited in the Middle Ages. Though the language of Donne and Drummond was far richer than the language of the Middle Ages, their thoughts were almost exactly similar to those of the earlier time. The disillusionment of the late Renaissance had caused a renewed emphasis on death as the beginning of true existence. Popular literature, having for a time expressed vital things, dropped them, and they were once more taken up by the specialists. Donne and Drummond, Burton, Browne and Jeremy Taylor, are the great writers on death in the next generation; vital emotion on the subject was no longer the possession of dramatic poetry; it had returned to religion.

Yet this specialization was, in the long run, not a defeat for the Renaissance but a victory. The fact that expression of thought about death in the later drama became empty and rhetorical may be taken to show, not only that the drama had degenerated, but that the vivid apprehension of death had faded from the common mind. Temporarily, to be sure, disillusion, in life as well as in drama, had apparently conquered: Donne tells us in one of his sermons that he met with seven diffident and dejected souls for one presumptuous one, and that as a pastor he had much exercise in raising dejected spirits.[20] But Donne and his congregation represented only one side of the picture, and it was the side that eventually was to grow dim. For by Donne's time the Renaissance emphasis on the present world had begun to find an outlet in a form that no longer had a direct connection with religion, and to which the thought of death was irrelevant. The heavens no longer revolved around a stationary earth, and the

20. See E. M. Simpson, *A Study of the Prose Works of John Donne*, Oxford, 1924, p. 119.

spiritual destiny of man was no longer the main business of the universe. As the seventeenth century progressed, the best minds turned more and more to nature rather than to the soul, and the externalization which is implied in the philosophy of Bacon became the chief legacy of the Renaissance. The internal development, the development through conflicting views of life and death, in the mind and the emotions, had reached its climax with Chapman and Shakespeare. In language, in thought, in technical accomplishment it had been expressed through a dramatic organization the greatness of which has not since been equalled, but which from its very nature could not last.

For the conditions behind that greatness were temporary. *Difficilisque in perfecto mora est naturaliterque quod procedere non potest recedit.* The intensity of the Elizabethan dramatic treatment of death was the result of a conflict between two views of man's nature which the ensuing development of scientific rationalism was to make impossible for many generations to come. And when literature next felt a need for emotional intensity about man's being, that essential conflict had disappeared: the poets of the Romantic movement, unlike the Elizabethan dramatists, were powerless to create tragedy.

INDEX

INDEX

Library
Auburn Community College
Auburn, N. Y.